W. H. Cooke

Church teaching for the Children of the Church

W. H. Cooke

Church teaching for the Children of the Church

ISBN/EAN: 9783337167592

Printed in Europe, USA, Canada, Australia, Japan

Cover: Foto ©ninafisch / pixelio.de

More available books at **www.hansebooks.com**

CHURCH TEACHING

FOR THE

CHILDREN OF THE CHURCH.

BY THE
REV. W. H. COOKE,
ASSISTANT MINISTER OF TRINITY PARISH, N. Y.

SIXTH EDITION, REVISED.

NEW YORK:
POTT, YOUNG & CO., COOPER UNION.
1872.

NOTE
TO THE
FIFTH AND IMPROVED EDITION.

Several changes have been made, and at the suggestion of a number of friends "the Church Catechism" has been inserted. It is proposed that one question from the "Church Catechism," be learned on each Sunday, with the lesson appointed, in order that it may constantly be brought before the minds of the children.

Grateful for the kind favor with which my effort has been received, I trust that the present additions and corrections may make this book more useful to those who are striving to educate the minds and hearts of the children of the Church.

W. H. C.

St. John's, Trinity Parish,
    Quinquagesima Sunday, 1871.

INTRODUCTORY.

Many among the Clergy as well as Superintendents of Sunday Schools have found it difficult, in large schools, to catechise their children, by reason of the great number and variety of text-books which were used to suit the comprehension of children of various age and ability. It is the design of this little book to meet, in a measure, this difficulty.

It contains simple questions which are within the comprehension of the youngest, and then are enlarged and amplified with the assistance of Scripture texts, so as to be sufficiently advanced for almost any child who attends school.

The Rector or Superintendent in catechising his children addresses himself therefore to the entire school, and not to a few who may chance to be in the same book. This advantage will enable him to interest the whole school at once, which he cannot do according to the accustomed use.

This, together with the fact that the truth which is taught is in absolute conformity with the teaching of the Church, in the order of the ecclesiastical year, will, we trust, recommend it to the kind consideration of Churchmen.

In order that the method may be understood, it will be well to read the following

DIRECTIONS TO TEACHERS.

Let all the scholars of the school be divided into four grades. The youngest should study only those questions marked 1.

Those of the second grade should learn 1 and 2.

Those of the third grade, 1, 2 and 3.

Those of the fourth grade, 1, 2, 3 and 4, or the whole.

It will thus be seen that it will take a child four years to complete the book, and when he has finished, he will have in his mind a vast store of heavenly wisdom. Of course each grade may be divided into as many classes as may be practicable.

May the Divine blessing attend this feeble effort.

St. John's, Trinity Parish, *Oct.* 1868.

OFFICES.

BEFORE SCHOOL.

Begin by singing a Psalm or Hymn.

Repeat the creed—

There shall be said a selection of one psalm from the psalter of the day.

V. The Lord be with you.

R. And with thy spirit.

Let us Pray.

V. O Lord, show Thy mercy upon us.
R. And grant us Thy salvation.
V. O God, make clean our hearts within us.
R. And take not Thy Holy Spirit from us.
Our Father who art in heaven, &c.

Then shall follow the Collect for the day, with such others from the Book of Common Prayer as the Superintendent may select, concluding with the following:

O Almighty God! whom, in our own strength, we are not able to serve and please, graciously behold us, thy unworthy servants, to whom Thou hast intrusted the work of teaching the young out of Thy Holy Word. May we ourselves be taught of the Spirit; and being filled with zeal for our work, may we prove faithful to the end, that so Thy name may be glorified, Thy church enlarged, and true religion and piety be established among us to all generations; through Jesus Christ our Lord. *Amen.*

O thou Gracious Bishop and Shepherd of Israel, tenderly regard these children, the lambs of Thy fold. Carry them in Thy bosom; cause them to know Thy voice, to obey Thy will, and to follow Thy steps. May they receive with meekness the engrafted word which is able to save their souls; and walking in the way of righteousness, may they grow in grace as members of Thy church on earth, while here they live; and when they die, may they be received into Thy fold in heaven, there to praise Thee, with the Father and the Holy Ghost, ever one God, world without end. *Amen.*

AFTER SCHOOL.

V. Like as a father pitieth his own children.

R. Even so is the Lord merciful unto them that fear Him.

V. Glory be to the Father, and to the Son, and to the Holy Ghost.

R. As it was in the beginning, is now, and ever shall be, world without end. *Amen.*

Here shall be sung a Psalm or Hymn.

Let us Pray.

Grant, we beseech Thee, Almighty God, that the words which we have heard this day with our outward ears, may, through Thy grace, be so grafted inwardly in our hearts, that they may bring forth in us the fruits of good living, to the honor and praise of Thy Name, through Jesus Christ our Lord. *Amen.*

The grace of our Lord Jesus Christ, and the love of God, and the fellowship of the Holy Ghost, be with us all evermore. *Amen.*

THE FIRST SUNDAY IN ADVENT.

The Collect.

ALMIGHTY God, give us grace that we may cast away the works of darkness, and put upon us the armour of light, now in the time of this mortal life, in which thy Son Jesus Christ came to visit us in great humility; that in the last day, when he shall come again in his glorious Majesty to judge both the quick and dead, we may rise to the life immortal, through him who liveth and reigneth with thee and the Holy Ghost, now and ever. *Amen.*

The Epistle. Rom. xiii. 8.—*The Gospel.* St. Matt. xxi. 1.

1. Q. What is Advent Sunday?
   A. The Christian New Year's day.
2. Q. Why does the Church begin the year at this time?
   A. Because at this time her Saviour, the true Sun of Righteousness, began to rise upon the world.
3. Q. Where is the prophecy in reference to the Sun of Righteousness?
   A. Malachi iv. 2.
4. Q. How does the righteousness of Christ affect us?
   A. Rom. v. 18.
1. Q. Who announced the coming of Christ?
   A. St. John the Baptist.
2. Q. Where did St. John preach?

A. In the wilderness of Judea, saying, "Repent ye; for the kingdom of heaven is at hand."
3. Q. Did Christ recognize St. John as his forerunner?
A. St. Matth. xi. 13, 14.
4. Q. Where was the prophecy, and how was it fulfilled, as to the word which St. John should speak?
A. Isaiah xl. 3; St. Matth. iii. 3.
1. Q. Where did our Saviour make his appearance?
A. At Jerusalem, the chief city of the Jews.
2. Q. Why did he go to Jerusalem?
A. Because, being the rightful Prince of the house of David, he went to the city in which his father had reigned as king.
3. Q. How did Christ announce his coming?
A. St. Matth. xxi. 5.
4. Q. What does the Prophet Isaiah say concerning his coming to Jerusalem?
A. Isaiah lxii. 11.
1. Q. Who accompanied Christ to Jerusalem?
A. His disciples, and a great multitude besides.
2. Q. What led them to go with him?
A. That they might hail him as their King.
3. Q. Did they expect him to rule over them like any other king?
A. Yes; as they interpreted all the prophecies in relation to his reigning over them, in a temporal and not a spiritual sense.
4. Q. What did Christ say of his kingdom?
A. St. John xviii. 36.

THE FIRST SUNDAY IN ADVENT.

Q. How did the Holy Jesus come?
A. In great humility.
Q. How was the humility of Christ manifested?
A. By his riding upon a beast universally regarded with contempt.
Q. Are we required to exercise ourselves in humility?
A. Col. iii. 12.
Q. What reward is promised to the humble?
A. St. Matth. xviii. 4; Jas. iv. 6; Prov. xxii. 4.
Q. How did the people receive their king?
A. They spread their garments and green branches in his path.
Q. With what words did they hail him?
A. "Hosanna to the Son of David—blessed is He that cometh in the name of the Lord—Hosanna in the highest."
Q. What after incident proved that the Jews were not sincere in their adulations?
A. St. Matth. xxvii. 23.
Q. Is an outward expression of reverence all that is required of us?
A. St. Matth. vii. 21.
Q. What are we taught by the action of our Saviour?
A. To humbly bear all that God may put upon us.
Q. Can we accomplish this by our own will and strength?
A. No; we must devoutly implore the assistance of his Holy Spirit, who will help our infirmities.

3. Q. In whose name must we ask God for assistance?
A. In the name of our Lord and Saviour Jesus Christ; who ever sitteth at the right hand of God to make intercession for us.
4. Q. Is there any promise in Scripture that if we so ask we shall receive?
A. St. John xiv. 13.
1. Q. To what does the Advent of Christ look forward?
A. To his second coming in glorious majesty.
2. Q. What will be the object of his Second Advent?
A. "To judge both the quick and the dead."
3. Q. Where is it said that Christ shall judge the world?
A. St. John v. 22.
4. Q. What will Christ say to those on his right and on his left hand at the day of judgment?
A. St. Matth. xxv. 34, 41.

"Awake—again the gospel trump is blown—
From year to year it swells with louder tone,
From year to year the signs of wrath
Are gathering round the Judge's path,
Strange words fulfilled, and mighty works achieved,
And truth in all the world both hated and believed."

Keble.

THE SECOND SUNDAY IN ADVENT.
The Collect.

BLESSED Lord, who hast caused all holy Scriptures to be written for our learning; Grant that we may in such wise hear them, read, mark, learn, and inwardly digest them, that by patience, and comfort of thy holy Word, we may embrace, and ever hold fast the blessed hope of everlasting life, which thou hast given us in our Saviour Jesus Christ. *Amen.*

The Epistle. Rom. xv. 4.—*The Gospel.* St. Luke xxi. 25.

1. Q. What are the Holy Scriptures?
   A. The written word of God.
2. Q. How was the Bible written?
   A. By holy men who were inspired of God.
3. Q. What two parts does the Bible embrace?
   A. The Old and New Testaments, called also the Law and the Gospel; the one being the foreshadow of the other.
4. Q. What is the difference between the Law and the Gospel?
   A. Rom. iii. 20; Rom. xvi. 25, 26.
1. Q. What do the Scriptures teach us of ourselves?
   A. That we are all great and miserable sinners.
2. Q. How came we to be so sinful by nature?
   A. Our first parents disobeyed the commands of God in eating of the forbidden tree in Eden, and we have by nature followed their example of disobedience.
3. Q. Are there none among men who are sinless?
   A. Ps. xiv. 3.
4. Q. Was there ever a man on earth who was perfectly sinless?
   A. Hebrews iv. 15.
1. Q. What is the result of our persistent wickedness?
   A. We must die and perish.
2. Q. How will we die and perish?

A. Our bodies will decay into dust, and our souls go to the place of punishment.
3. Q. Where are we told that our bodies will decay?
A. Gen. iii. 19.
4. Q. Where is it said that the souls of the wicked shall perish?
A. Ezek. xviii. 4.
1. Q. Can we prevent our death?
A. No; for this is the penalty of our natural sin.
2. Q. What do we mean by natural sin?
A. That which has descended to us as a result of the fall of Adam.
3. Q. Are there any instances recorded in the Bible of those who did not see death?
A. 2 Kings ii. 11; Heb. xi. 5.
4. Q. By Adam's sin death comes to all; how then can we avoid the consequences of death?
A. 1 Cor. xv. 21, 22.
1. Q. Does the Bible tell us how we may avoid eternal misery?
A. Yes; by believing on our Saviour Jesus Christ.
2. Q. What does believing in Christ include?
A. Faith in him and following his commands.
3. Q. Can Faith and Works be separated?
A. St. Jas. ii. 22.
4. Q. What is the power which should influence us to faith and good works?
A. 2 Cor. v. 14, 15.
1. Q. How may we learn how to believe in our Saviour?

THE SECOND SUNDAY IN ADVENT.

A. The Bible tells us what we ought to do, and gives us the example of Christ to follow.

2. Q. How are we to know what the Bible teaches?
A. By listening to the voice of the Church, which is "the pillar and witness of the Truth."

3. Q. What does St. Paul lay down as the principal doctrines of the Gospel?
A. Heb. vi. 1, 2.

4. Q. What is the catalogue of virtues which St. Peter tells us we must add to our Faith?
A. 2 Peter i. 5-8.

1. Q. What does Scripture tell us will happen if we do not love and follow our Saviour?
A. We shall go to a place where we shall always be unhappy.

2. Q. How is this place described in Scripture?
A. As "a lake which burneth with fire and brimstone, where the Devil and false prophet are, in torment forever."

3. Q. In what consists the punishment of hell?
A. 2 Thess. i. 9.

4. Q. Will this punishment ever come to an end?
A. Rev. xiv. 11.

1. Q. What then should we always seek to do?
A. To follow the example of Christ in all things, that so we may dwell with Him forever.

2. Q. Is it possible to follow Christ in all things?
A. No; but we may strive to do so, by the grace of God, and this endeavor will be accepted, though it be an imperfect service.

3. Q. The temptations to sin are very great; is it therefore impossible to obey the commands of Christ?
A. 1 Cor. x. 13.
4. Q. What does St. Paul say of himself and all who are faithful unto death?
A. 2 Tim. iv. 7, 8.

"She has a charm, a word of fire,
A pledge of love that cannot tire;
By tempests, earthquakes, and by wars,
By rushing waves and falling stars,
By every sign her Lord foretold,
She sees the world is waxing old,
And through that last and direst storm
Descries by faith her Saviour's form."

Keble.

THE THIRD SUNDAY IN ADVENT.

The Collect.

O LORD Jesus Christ, who at thy first coming didst send thy messenger to prepare thy way before thee; Grant that the ministers and stewards of thy mysteries may likewise so prepare and make ready thy way, by turning the hearts of the disobedient to the wisdom of the just, that at thy second coming to judge the world we may be found an acceptable people in thy sight, who livest and reignest with the Father and the Holy Spirit, ever one God, world without end.

Amen.

The Epistle. 1 Cor. iv. 1.—*The Gospel.* St. Matt. xi. 2.

1. Q. Who heralded the first advent of Christ?
A. St. John the Baptist.

2. Q. How did St. John prepare the way for the coming of Christ?
A. By directing their attention to him, and showing them how the prophecies were fulfilled in him.
3. Q. How did St. John know who the Messiah was?
A. Matt. xi. 4, 5.
4. Q. What did St. John say of our Saviour?
A. St. John i. 27.
1. Q. Who announce the second advent of Christ?
A. The ministers of the Gospel.
2. Q. Who were the first ministers of the Gospel?
A. The twelve Apostles, who preached the words which they heard their Master utter.
3. Q. Who were next selected by our Saviour to preach the glad tidings?
A. St. Luke x. 1.
4. Q. Did our Saviour, who is the head of the Church, take upon himself the office of the ministry?
A. Heb. v. 5.
1. Q. By whom were the ministers sent?
A. By Christ himself.
2. Q. How are ministers now sent by our Saviour?
A. Through the Bishops, who were authorized by Christ to perpetuate the ministry.
3. Q. What are the words of the commission to serve Christ in the ministry?
A. St. Matt. xxviii. 19.
4. Q. What proof have we that this divine commission is necessary?

A. Heb. v. 4.

1. Q. How many kinds or orders of ministers did Christ send?
A. Three: Bishops, Priests, and Deacons.
2. Q. What were the first Bishops called?
A. Apostles, which title was reserved to distinguish those who were personally appointed by Christ.
3. Q. How do you prove, from Scripture, that the Apostles had power to send ministers as Christ had sent them?
A. St. John xx. 21.
4. Q. Can you give any Scripture instances of such consecration?
A. 1 Tim. v. 22; Tit. i. 5.
1. Q. For what were ministers sent?
A. To preach the gospel and to administer the Holy Sacraments.
2. Q. How many gospels are there?
A. Four, or rather one gospel, according to St. Matthew, St. Mark, St. Luke, and St. John.
3. Q. What is the object of the Acts of the Holy Apostles?
A. To teach us of the establishment of the visible Church of Christ.
4. Q. What are the Epistles?
A. They are the explanations of the various doctrines contained in the gospel, with exhortations to believe and obey them, and are designed to apply to all men, as well as to those to whom they were sent.

THE THIRD SUNDAY IN ADVENT.

1. Q. What is it to preach the gospel?
   A. To proclaim and explain the word of God.
2. Q. How is this to be done?
   A. By revealing the word of God as it is received by the Holy Catholic Church.
3. Q. Why should we rely upon the voice of the Church in the interpretation of Scripture?
   A. 2 Peter i. 20.
4. Q. Are we not all, in a certain sense, commanded to do the work of ministers?
   A. 1 Peter iv. 10.

1. Q. What is it to administer the Holy Sacraments?
   A. To apply the visible means of grace which Christ gave us.
2. Q. What are these visible means of Grace?
   A. Baptism and the Lord's Supper, which the Church teaches are sacraments "generally necessary to Salvation."
3. Q. How do we know that Baptism is designed for our assistance towards Salvation?
   A. St. John iii. 5.
4. Q. Where are we assured of the benefit of the eucharistic feast?
   A. St. John vi. 56, 57.

1. Q. What is the great object of the administration of the Word and Sacraments?
   A. To warn and to assist us "to flee from the wrath to come."
2. Q. How long a time is given us to prepare for the judgment?

A. Our natural life; for after death there is neither time nor place for repentance.

3. Q. What does our Saviour say of his work, which equally applies to the work of our salvation?
A. St. John ix. 4.

4. Q. How do we know that all our actions will be judged by God?
A. Eccles. xii. 14.

"Go preach my gospel," saith the Lord,
"Bid the whole earth my grace receive;
Explain to them my sacred word,
Bid them believe, obey, and live."

Hy. 98.

THE FOURTH SUNDAY IN ADVENT.

The Collect.

O LORD, raise up, we pray thee, thy power, and come among us, and with great might succor us; that whereas, through our sins and wickedness, we are sore let and hindered in running the race that is set before us, thy bountiful grace and mercy may speedily help and deliver us; through the satisfaction of thy SON our Lord, to whom, with thee and the HOLY GHOST, be honor and glory, world without end. *Amen.*

The Epistle. Phil. iv. 4.—*The Gospel.* St. John i. 19.

1. Q. What is the Second Advent of Christ?
A. His coming in judgment at the last day.

2. Q. What is meant by Christ's coming in judgment?
A. His presence for a second time in the flesh, to examine the actions of men, and pronounce their reward or punishment.

3. Q. How do we know that Christ will judge the world?
A. St. John v. 22.
4. Q. Who will sit with Christ in the capacity of judges?
A. St. Matthew xix. 28.
1. Q. Will this judgment be general?
A. Yes; every one who ever lived, from Adam down, will be judged.
2. Q. How does reason suggest a general judgment?
A. The practice of virtue or vice produces in the mind either contentment or remorse, and this sensibility suggests future rewards and punishments.
3. Q. What does Job say of the wicked who prosper in this world?
A. Job xxi. 30.
4. Q. What does the Preacher say of those who follow the inclinations of their evil hearts?
A. Eccles. xi. 9.
1. Q. How do the Scriptures assure us of a judgment?
A. Our Saviour distinctly portrays the scenes of the judgment.
2. Q. What does St. Paul tell us?
A. "We shall all stand before the judgment seat of Christ."
3. Q. What assurance has God given us of a general judgment?
A. Acts xvii. 31.
4. Q. How will the judgment come?

A. 2 Pet. iii. 10.
1. Q. When will the judgment be?
A. At the end of the world.
2. Q. Why is the judgment reserved till the end of the world?
A. That all may hear our sentence, whether it be of reward or punishment.
3. Q. When we die do we go immediately into the place of happiness or misery?
A. Yes; but it is not until after the resurrection, when the body is joined with the soul, that we shall receive our full reward or punishment.
4. Q. What is the ground of this belief?
A. As the body is partaker of the righteousness or sin of the soul, so it must partake of the reward or punishment, which cannot transpire until after the resurrection and day of judgment.
1. Q. Why will the Lord Jesus Christ judge the world?
A. That He who was despised, may be honored before men.
2. Q. How will he be thus honored?
A. *He* will be the Judge, who himself once stood before a human tribunal as a criminal.
3. Q. What is the reason of this exaltation of our Saviour?
A. Philip. ii. 8, 9.

THE FOURTH SUNDAY IN ADVENT.

4. Q. What does Isaiah prophesy of his glory in that day?
   A. Isa. xl. 5.
1. Q. Who will be judged on that day?
   A. All angels and men, from the greatest to the meanest.
2. Q. For what shall we be judged?
   A. For the deeds done here in the body, whether they be good or bad.
3. Q. Will all receive equal reward or punishment?
   A. 1 Cor. xv. 41.
4. Q. What will be the standard by which we shall be judged?
   A. St. Luke xii. 47, 48.
1. Q. Is the time of our Saviour's coming fixed?
   A. No; it is one of the secrets of God.
2. Q. Did not our Saviour give a general idea of when the judgment should be?
   A. He said that there should be signs; but as man, he did not know the exact time.
3. Q. How do you prove this?
   A. St. Mark xiii. 32.
4. Q. What should we be looking for at his coming?
   A. Titus ii. 13.
1. Q. What does the certainty of the judgment teach us?
   A. That we should prepare to meet our Judge.
2. Q. How can we make this preparation?
   A. By improving all those talents which God has intrusted to us.

3. Q. What does the uncertainty of the time of judgment suggest?
A. St. Matt. xxiv. 44.
4. Q. What assurance of our Saviour should encourage us to make this preparation?
A. 2 Pet. iii. 9.

"Great God, what do I see and hear!
　The end of things created:
The Judge of man I see appear,
　On clouds of glory seated.
The trumpet sounds, the graves restore
　The dead which they contained before;
　Prepare, my soul, to meet him."

Hy. 194.

CHRISTMAS-DAY.

The Collect.

ALMIGHTY God, who hast given us thy only-begotten Son to take our nature upon him, and as at this time to be born of a pure virgin; Grant that we being regenerate, and made thy children by adoption and grace, may daily be renewed by thy Holy Spirit; through the same our Lord Jesus Christ, who liveth and reigneth with thee and the same Spirit, ever one God, world without end. *Amen.*

The Epistle. Heb. i. 1.—*The Gospel.* St. John i. 1.

1. Q. What day is this?
A. The birthday of our Saviour.
2. Q. What is our authority for celebrating Christmas on December 25th?

A. The authority of the Primitive Church, and its observance by all Christians since the time of our Saviour.
3. Q. When does St. Luke date the birth of Christ?
A. St. Luke ii. 1, 2.
4. Q. Is it really of importance on what day we celebrate the nativity?
A. Not if we set apart some particular day for the expression of our gratitude and devotion for this greatest of all blessings.
1. Q. How does the Church celebrate Christmas?
A. By her beautiful services.
2. Q. What external mark of joy is universally adopted?
A. The green boughs with which we decorate our churches.
3. Q. What authority have we for this custom in the Old Testament?
A. Isai. lx. 13.
4. Q. Relate a like expression of joy in the New Testament.
A. St. John xii. 12, 13.
1. Q. Who was the mother of our Saviour?
A. The Virgin Mary, of the house and lineage of David.
2. Q. To whom was the B. V. Mary espoused?
A. To Joseph, a carpenter, who was also of the family of David.
3. Q. What sign did Isaiah predict of the birth of our Saviour?

A. Isai. vii. 14.
4. Q. What was the exclamation of Mary when she knew who her son was to be?
A. St. Luke i. 46, 47, 48.
1. Q. Where was Jesus Christ born?
A. In Bethlehem, six miles south of Jerusalem.
2. Q. At what place in Bethlehem?
A. In a lowly manger, surrounded by cattle; as there was no room for his parents at the inn.
3. Q. Why was Bethlehem called the city of David?
A. 1 Sam. xvii. 12.
4. Q. Where is it foretold that Christ should be born at Bethlehem?
A. Micah v. 2.
1. Q. What does Christmas teach us?
A. That Christ was man as well as God.
2. Q. Of what does his royal descent assure us?
A. That as David his father was the temporal king of the chosen people of God, so Christ is the spiritual king.
3. Q. What prophecy predicts the incarnation?
A. Isai. ix. 6.
4. Q. What was the testimony of St. John?
A. St. John i. 14.
1. Q. Who published to the world the birth of our Saviour?
A. The Angel of the Lord, to the shepherds who were feeding their flocks by night.
2. Q. How did the angel dissipate the terror of the shepherds?

A. By announcing that in the city of David a Saviour was born which is Christ the Lord.

3. Q. By what sign did the angel tell them to recognize Christ?
A. St. Luke ii. 12.

4. Q. At this news, what did the angel and heavenly host say?
A. St. Luke ii. 14.

1. Q. What does Christmas mean?
A. The mass, or prayer or service to Christ.

2. Q. What has it always been esteemed?
A. The greatest of all our festivals, and celebrated from Apostolic times to this day.

3. Q. Is this gift of God, in his Son, designed to be bestowed on all men?
A. St. John iii. 16.

4. Q. What then should we exclaim, in acknowledgment of this inestimable gift?
A. 2 Cor. ix. 15.

"The first Noel an angel sung,
The carol of an angel tongue,
While shepherds watching o'er the night,
Heard both the song, and saw the light.
 Noel, Noel,
Born is the King of Israel.

In gentle bands the infant lay,
In manger, 'mid the corn and hay;
The Son of David's royal line
Was born within the stalls for kine.
 Noel, Noel,
Born is the King of Israel."
   From an " Olden Composure."

THE SUNDAY AFTER CHRISTMAS-DAY.

The Collect.

ALMIGHTY God, who hast given us thy only-begotten Son to take our nature upon him, and as at this time to be born of a pure virgin; Grant that we being regenerate, and made thy children by adoption and grace, may daily be renewed by thy Holy Spirit; through the same our Lord Jesus Christ, who liveth and reigneth with thee and the same Spirit, ever one God, world without end. *Amen.*

The Epistle. Gal. iv. 1.—*The Gospel.* St. Matt. 1. 18.

1. Q. What do we first learn from the circumstances of the Nativity?
   A. That Christ came in poverty to redeem even the poorest.
2. Q. To whom, therefore, was his birth first announced?
   A. To the simple shepherds of Bethlehem.
3. Q. What comfort is here suggested to the humblest?
   A. Isaiah xxix. 19.
4. Q. How is the mercy of God manifested through the poverty of Christ?
   A. 2 Cor. viii. 9.
1. Q. Did the Jews look for the birth of Christ?
   A. Yes; but they did not expect him to come in poverty.
2. Q. How general was the belief of the appearance of a great deliverer?

A. Suetonius says that throughout the East the belief was general that an universal ruler should come out of Judea."
3. Q. What is the testimony of Tacitus?
A. "That it was contained in the ancient books of the priests, that the governors of the world should come out of Judea."
4. Q. How does this testimony harmonize with the prophet Micah?
A. Mic. v. 2.
1. Q. What was the principal office of our Saviour?
A. To make known to man the will of God.
2. Q. How was this to be attained?
A. By coming into the world and mingling with those to whom he brought the glad tidings.
3. Q. What was this will of God?
A. St. John vi. 40.
4. Q. What is the result if this will of God be despised?
A. John iii. 36.
1. Q. How was Christ peculiarly fitted to make known the will of God?
A. By the dignity and excellency of his person.
2. Q. How did our Saviour's dignity assist him in his mission?
A. As proceeding directly from the bosom of the Father, and being one with him.
3. Q. How do we know that this intimate communion existed between the Father and the Son?
A. John iii. 34.

3*

4. Q. Did this union embrace all the properties of God?
A. Col. ii. 9.
1. Q. Mention another qualification of our Saviour for his work?
A. His ability in expressing his doctrines and precepts.
2. Q. In what consists the perfection of his doctrines?
A. The clearness with which they reveal all that is necessary for the welfare and happiness of man.
3. Q. Of what do the precepts of our Saviour remind us?
A. Of all the duties which we owe to God, our neighbor, and ourselves.
4. Q. How has Christ summed up these duties?
A. Matt xxii. 37, 38, 39, 40.
1. Q. How did the blessed Jesus enforce his principles?
A. By the brightness of his example.
2. Q. Did he use no force in bringing men to him?
A. No other than the force of love.
3. Q. What did he recommend those who came unto him to do?
A. St. Matth. xi. 29.
4. Q. What testimony does St. Peter give of the purity and consistency of his example?
A. 1 Pet. ii. 22, 23.
1. Q. What power had our Saviour which gave force to his work?
A. Assistance by grace and precious promises of reward.

2. Q. What was this grace which Christ bestowed?
    A. His Holy Spirit; which afterwards was to be conveyed by means of the lawful administration of his holy Sacrament.
3. Q. What was St. Paul's testimony as to the sufficiency of that grace?
    A. 2 Cor. xii. 9.
4. Q. Is it impossible to attain the promises without the assistance of Christ?
    A. St. John xv. 5.
1. Q. What then should be our great feeling at Christmas-tide?
    A. That of thankfulness for the love of God manifested in Christ.
2. Q. How should we express this thankfulness?
    A. By imitating the infinite love of our Saviour, and following his glorious example.
3. Q. How may we abuse this festive season?
    A. When we make an external display of joy, and do not embrace and hold fast the blessed hope which is given us in our Saviour Christ.
4. Q. How do we know that the promised benefits of Christ's incarnation will be realized?
    A. Rom. viii. 32.

"O Thou who keep'st the key of Love,
Open thy fount, Eternal Dove,
And overflow this heart of mine,
Enlarging as it fills with Thee,
Till in one blaze of charity,
Care and remorse are lost, like motes in light divine."

Keble.

THE CIRCUMCISION OF CHRIST.

The Collect.

ALMIGHTY God, who madest thy blessed Son to be circumcised, and obedient to the Law for man; Grant us the true Circumcision of the Spirit; that, our hearts, and all our members, being mortified from all worldly and carnal lusts, we may in all things obey thy blessed will; through the same thy Son Jesus Christ our Lord. *Amen.*

The Epistle. Rom. iv. 8.—*The Gospel.* St. Luke ii. 15.

1. Q. When do we celebrate the festival of the circumcision?
   A. Eight days after Christmas, when our Saviour received his name.
2. Q. What was circumcision?
   A. The rite by which Jewish children were received into the Church of God.
3. Q. What penalty attached to those who were not circumcised?
   A. Gen. xvii. 14.
4. Q. With whom was the covenant of circumcision first made?
   A. Gen. xvii. 10.
1. Q. What was the original design of circumcision?
   A. As a sign that they should inherit the land of promise.
2. Q. Why should it have been made visible?

A. To remind them to strive after the invisible grace which would make them inheritors of heaven.
3. Q. Upon whom was the rite of circumcision binding?
A. Upon all the Jews throughout the world who lived before Christ.
4. Q. Why is it not binding now?
A. Because our Saviour, who is the head of the Church, has substituted another form of admission into his Church.
1. Q. What was it that Christ substituted for circumcision?
A. Baptism, at which time our Christian name is given.
2. Q. Upon whom is baptism to be administered?
A. On all who desire to enter into the covenant of grace.
3. Q. Was outward circumcision all that was required?
A. Deut. xxx. 6.
4. Q. If a person is baptized, will that alone save him?
A. St. Luke xiii. 3.
1. Q. What may we learn from the circumcision of Jesus?
A. That infants are to be admitted to the covenant by baptism.
2. Q. Was the custom of infant baptism primitive?
A. Throughout the early Church we read of it, from the time of the Apostles.
3. Q. What argument does our Saviour seem to use?

    A. St. Matth. xix. 14.
4. Q. What other argument is suggested in Scripture
    A. St. John iii. 5.
1. Q. What name was given to our Saviour?
    A. The name of Jesus.
2. Q. What does this name mean?
    A. Saviour, because he came to save them which were lost.
3. Q. Who gave Christ his name?
    A. St. Luke ii. 21.
4. Q. Who gave you your name?
    A. "My sponsors in baptism, wherein I was made a member of Christ, the Child of God, and an inheritor of the kingdom of heaven."
1. Q. Why was our Saviour circumcised, seeing that he was sinless?
    A. In order that, being under the law, he might redeem us from the law.
2. Q. Why did he obey the whole law?
    A. To set us an example of obedience, that we might be perfect in all things.
3. Q. How did circumcision help the Jew spiritually?
    A. It assisted him in cutting off, or renouncing all evil passions and offences against God.
4. Q. What does baptism do for the true believer?
    A. It aids him in mortifying all carnal and ungodly lusts.
1. Q. Can we perfectly obey God without being baptized?
    A. No; for our Saviour has directly commanded it.

2. Q. What is the outward sign in baptism?
A. "Water, wherein the person is baptized in the name of the Father, Son, and Holy Ghost."
3. Q. What inward work does it signify?
A. A death unto sin, and a life unto righteousness.
4. Q. What, therefore, does St. Peter say?
A. Acts ii. 38.
1. Q. Did the promise of the descent of the Holy Ghost at baptism include children?
A. St. Peter says, "to you and to your children."
2. Q. What then is our duty?
A. To receive the little lambs into our arms as Jesus did.
3. Q. Baptism frees us from the bondage of the law; what, therefore, should we strive to remember on this festival?
A. Gal. v. 1.
4. Q. What should we do if we really possess the spirit of God?
A. Gal. v. 25.

"By blood and water too
   God's mark is set on thee,
That in Thee every faithful view
   Both covenants might see.

If thou would'st reap in love,
   First sow in holy fear;
So life a winter's morn may prove
   To a bright endless year."

Keble.

THE EPIPHANY.

The Collect.

O GOD, who by the leading of a star didst manifest thy only-begotten Son to the Gentiles; Mercifully grant that we, who know thee now by faith, may after this life have the fruition of thy glorious Godhead; through JESUS CHRIST our Lord. *Amen.*

The Epistle. Ephes. iii. 1 — *The Gospel.* St. Matt. ii. 1.

1. Q. What festival is celebrated on the 6th of Jan.?
   A. The Epiphany, or the manifestation of Christ to the Gentiles.
2. Q. What then was revealed?
   A. A Saviour, who would introduce the gentile world into a covenant from which they were excluded by the Jewish law.
3. Q. Where are we told that the Gentiles should have equal privileges with the Jews?
   A. Ephes. iii. 6.
4. Q. Who was the great Apostle to the Gentiles?
   A. Ephes. iii. 1, 2.
1. Q. How was Christ manifested to the Gentiles?
   A. By being manifested to the wise men of the East, who represented them.
2. Q. Who were these wise men?
   A. They were called Magi, a name given by the Persians to Priests, wise men, and philosophers.
3. Q. What was the custom of the Magi?
   A. To study the heavens very diligently.

THE EPIPHANY.

4. Q. What arrested their attention at this time?
A. A peculiar luminary in the heavens, which led them to expect some great event, such as the birth of a great man.
1. Q. What was the luminary which attracted the Magi.
A. The Star in the East.
2. Q. Were they expecting the appearance of this Star?
A. Yes; they were watching for some kind of remarkable appearance in the heavens.
3. Q. What prophecy led them to expect it?
A. Numbers xxiv. 17.
4. Q. What evidence is there that this prophecy referred to the Epiphany Star?
A. Rev. xxii. 16.
1. Q. Where did the Star guide the wise men?
A. It went before them till it stood over the place where Jesus lay.
2. Q. To whom did they apply for information?
A. To Herod, the King of Judea, who sent to inquire of the Scribes and Chief Priests.
3. Q. What answer did they make to Herod?
A. Matth. ii. 5, 6.
4. Q. What did Herod command the Magi to do?
A. Matth. ii. 8.
1. Q. What did the wise men do when they saw the Holy Child?
A. They fell down and worshipped Him.
2. Q. What was the position of worship among the Orientals?

A. Prostration, or falling at full length with the face to the ground.

3. Q. Did they return to Herod to tell of their success?
A. St. Matth. ii. 12.

4. Q. What evidence have we that Herod was not sincere in his expressed desire to worship Christ with the wise men?
A. St. Matth. ii. 16.

1. Q. What did the Magi bring with them?
A. Gifts, which they presented to the Holy Child.

2. Q. What were these gifts?
A. Gold, frankincense, and myrrh, the choicest products of their country.

3. Q. What gifts are we expected to make to Christ?
A. Psa. li. 17.

4. Q. What external sacrifice does St. Paul suggest as pleasing to God?
A. Heb. xiii. 16.

1. Q. Is Christ manifested to all the Gentiles?
A. No; many millions have not as yet heard of him.

2. Q. Who are the Gentiles now?
A. All whom we call the heathen, and who have never received the good news of the gospel.

3. Q. What prophecy is being fulfilled by the efforts of Christians?
A. Mal. i. 11.

4. Q. What promise of our Saviour encourages us to hope that this knowledge will be universal?
A. St. Matth. xxviii. 20.

FIRST SUNDAY AFTER THE EPIPHANY.

1. Q. What then is our duty?
   A. To send missionaries to teach and baptize the heathen.
2. Q. How is this to be accomplished?
   A. By the liberal contributions of those who have felt the value and love of Christ.
3. Q. How has St. Paul represented the necessity of missionary action among Christians?
   A. Rom. x. 14, 15.
4. Q. What does our Saviour say of him who has received much?
   A. St. Luke xii. 48.

"Now by a strange and sudden Star,
Three wise men went their way afar;
And journey'd on with deep intent
To seek a king, where'er it went.

The Star, their guide 'twixt North and West,
O'er Bethlehem's walls at length took rest;
And here its light in one calm stay,
Fell o'er the place where Jesus lay.

These wise men three, with offerings meet,
Fall down and worship Jesus' feet;
With offerings rich, the gift of old,
Rare myrrh, and frankincense and gold."
From an Olden Composure.

THE FIRST SUNDAY AFTER THE EPIPHANY.

The Collect.

O LORD, we beseech thee mercifully to receive the prayers of thy people who call upon thee; and grant that they may both perceive and know what things they ought to do, and also may have grace and power faithfully to fulfil the same; through Jesus Christ our Lord. *Amen.*

The Epistle. Rom. xii. 1.—*The Gospel.* St. Luke ii. 41.

1. Q. Where did our Saviour pass his early days?
   A. At Nazareth, a city in Galilee.
2. Q. How long did Christ dwell in Nazareth?
   A. Until he commenced his public ministry, or about thirty years.
3. Q. Why did our Saviour dwell at Nazareth, instead of Bethlehem, where he was born?
   A. St. Matth. ii. 23.
4. Q. Where is Christ called a Nazarene in the Old Testament?
   A. As the word Nazarene signified a slighted and despised person, it may be said that several of the Prophets so represented Christ, as for example, Isaiah liii. 3.
1. Q. How old was Jesus when his parents took him to Jerusalem?
   A. He was twelve years old.
2. Q. What did they go to Jerusalem for at this time?
   A. To be present at the feast of the Passover.
3. Q. What were the three great festivals of the Jews?
   A. The Passover, Pentecost, and Feast of Tabernacles; with which Easter, Whit-Sunday, and Christmas correspond in the Christian Church.
4. Q. Where do you find the record of the institution of the Passover?
   A. Exod. xii. 1–14.

FIRST SUNDAY AFTER THE EPIPHANY.

1. Q. Did Jesus return with his father and mother when they left Jerusalem?
   A. No; he remained to talk with the Doctors in the Temple.
2. Q. Where did his parents suppose him to be?
   A. Somewhere in the company or caravan in which they were travelling.
3. Q. What was the effect of the conversation of Jesus?
   A. St. Luke ii. 47.
4. Q. In what posture did the persons instructed present themselves to the Jewish Doctors?
   A. Acts xxii. 3.
1. Q. Did this act of our Saviour show a lack of respect to his parents?
   A. No; because he had a great work to perform which they did not understand.
2. Q. How do we know that they did not understand his true character?
   A. Because they were astonished, and asked him why he was there.
3. Q. What answer did he make to their inquiries?
   A. St. Luke ii. 49.
4. Q. Did they understand this answer?
   A. St. Luke ii. 50.
1. Q. What may children learn by the action of Christ in the Temple?
   A. To begin early to serve the Lord.
2. Q. Does this conflict with parental authority?

A. No; for no authority is superior to God's law and parents have no right to demand anything which is contrary to it.
3. Q. What encouragement have our parents to bring up their children in the service of God?
A. Prov. xxii. 6.
4. Q. What assurance have children that their service will be accepted by God?
A. Prov. viii. 17.
1. Q. How did Christ prove his obedience to his parents?
A. He went with them to Nazareth, and was subject to them.
2. Q. What does this teach us?
A. To be obedient in all things to our parents.
3. Q. What command was given by Moses in relation to the obedience of children?
A. Exod. xx. 12.
4. Q. What does St. Paul say of this command?
A. Eph. vi. 2.
1. Q. What else do we know of our Saviour's childhood?
A. Nothing but that he grew in wisdom and stature, and in favor with God and man.
2. Q. When does the next account of him begin?
A. At his baptism by St. John.
3. Q. How should we grow in order to be like Christ?
A. 2 St. Pet. iii. 18.
4. Q. To whom will God give this grace?
A. Psa. lxxxiv. 11.

SECOND SUNDAY AFTER THE EPIPHANY.

1. Q. How shall we obtain grace to follow our Saviour?
   A. By humble and earnest prayer.
2. Q. For what do we pray in the collect for to-day?
   A. That we may learn our duty, and have grace to do it.
3. Q. What does St. Paul tell us we must do?
   A. Rom. xii. 2.
4. Q. How do we know that God will give us strength to perform this duty?
   A. Psa. cxlv. 18, 19.

"Jesus, when a little child,
   Taught us what we ought to be;
Holy, harmless, undefiled,
   Was the Saviour's infancy;
All the Father's glory shone
   In the person of His Son.

In his heavenly Father's house,
   Jesus spent his early days;
There he paid his solemn vows,
   There proclaimed his Father's praise;
Thus it was his lot to gain
   Favor both with God and man."

THE SECOND SUNDAY AFTER THE EPIPHANY.

The Collect.

ALMIGHTY and everlasting God, who dost govern all things in heaven and earth; Mercifully hear the supplications of thy people, and grant us thy peace all the days of our life; through Jesus Christ our Lord. *Amen.*

The Epistle. Rom. xii. 6.—*The Gospel.* St. John ii. 1.

1. Q. What is the first thing we read of in connection with Christ's ministry?
   A. His baptism by St. John the Baptist.
2. Q. Where was he baptized?
   A. In the river Jordan.
3. Q. What remarkable voice proclaimed the character of Jesus at the time of his baptism?
   A. St. Luke iii. 22.
4. Q. At what other time did this voice come to the ears of Christ?
   A. St. John xii. 28.
1. Q. What followed immediately after the baptism of Christ?
   A. He was led into the wilderness to be tempted.
2. Q. By whom was our Saviour led into the wilderness?
   A. By the Holy Spirit, in order that, as he came to overcome sin, he might overcome Satan, who was the cause of all human misery.
3. Q. What was our Saviour's preparation for this temptation?
   A. St. Matt. iv. 2.
4. Q. When did our Saviour say was the time when his disciples should fast?
   A. St. Matt. ix. 15.
1. Q. How did the Devil tempt Jesus?

SECOND SUNDAY AFTER THE EPIPHANY.

    A. First by calling upon him to show forth his miraculous power.
2. Q. In what way did he ask him to show this power?
    A. When he was hungered, to turn the stones into bread, for his refreshment.
3. Q. What Scripture did Satan quote in connection with the second temptation?
    A. Psalm xci. 11, 12.
4. Q. With what quotation did Jesus answer Satan in the third temptation?
    A. Deut. x. 20.
1. Q. Did Christ ever manifest his power by miracles?
    A. Yes; he began performing miracles at the marriage in Cana of Galilee.
2. Q. What was the nature of this miracle?
    A. The turning of water into wine.
3. Q. Wherein consisted the propriety of this miracle as an introduction to the work of Jesus?
    A. As a type of the "turning of the water of earth into the wine of heaven."
4. Q. How did St. Peter say that Christ was approved of God?
    A. Acts ii. 22.
1. Q. What is a miracle?
    A. A work which plainly signifies the power of God.
2. Q. How many of our Lord's miracles are recorded in the gospels?
    A. Thirty-three; although we may infer that he performed many more in the course of his charitable ministry.

3. Q. Give me an instance where one of the Apostles performed a miracle by the authority and power of Christ?
A. Acts iii. 6.

4. Q. Did Jesus predict that pretenders should follow him who would profess to perform miracles?
A. St. Matt. xxiv. 24.

1. Q. What was the object of the miracles of Christ?
A. To show his glory and mercy.

2. Q. What was this glory?
A. The glory of divinity, by which power he worked his miracles.

3. Q. What does St. John say in reference to the glory of our blessed Lord?
A. St. John i. 14.

4. Q. In what should we glory?
A. Jer. ix. 24.

1. Q. What was the effect of this manifestation of Christ's power at Cana of Galilee?
A. His disciples believed on him.

2. Q. What miracle will Jesus work in us, if we ask him?
A. He will transform us into holy beings, as he turned the water into wine.

3. Q. Is every man so transformed before he can be a true Christian?
A. 2 Cor. v. 17.

4. Q. How are we to obtain this gift of transformation?
A. St. Matt. vii. 8.

1. Q. What will be the result of this miracle wrought in us?
A. We shall receive that peace for which we pray in the Collect.
2. Q. What do you mean by this peace of God?
A. That firm assurance which is granted us with the knowledge that our sins, for Christ's sake, are forgiven.
3. Q. What assurance have the righteous that this peace will be bestowed?
A. Psalm cxix. 165; Philip. iv. 7.
4. Q. What benediction did our Saviour pronounce upon his disciples at the time that he promised them the Comforter, the Holy Ghost?
A. St. John xiv. 27.

As by thy power in Galilee
  "The modest water blush'd to see its Lord,"
So teach me in humility
  To turn my ear to Thy most Holy Word.
O blessed Lord, with pow'r divine,
  Work in my heart the miracle of grace,
That I may be entirely Thine;
  Be filled with thy life and joy and peace.

THE THIRD SUNDAY AFTER THE EPIPHANY.

The Collect.

ALMIGHTY and everlasting God, mercifully look upon our infirmities, and in all our dangers and necessities stretch forth thy right hand to help and defend us; through Jesus Christ our Lord. *Amen.*

The Epistle. Rom. xii. 16.—*The Gospel.* St. Matt. viii. 1.

1. Q. What is the striking feature in the gospel for this day?
A. Our Lord's mercy to the Roman Centurion, who was a Gentile.
2. Q. Why is this act striking?
A. Because the Jews had always considered themselves as the only nation on whom God would bestow mercy.
3. Q. Where do you find an intimation in prophecy that Christ would extend his mercy to the Gentiles?
A. Isaiah xlix. 6.
4. Q. What is the testimony of Christ to this fact?
A. St. Matt. viii. 11.
1. Q. In what consists the peculiarity, of this miracle?
A. That our Lord, in his ministry thus showed his power to the Gentiles?
2. Q. What did he teach them by this act?
A. To rely on his power for protection, rather than on their false gods.
3. Q. Did he design also to show the Gentiles that they were to be admitted to spiritual privileges?
A. St. John x. 16.
4. Q. What subsequent act proves that our Saviour designed this covenant to be continued?
A. St. Matt. xxviii. 19, first clause.
1. Q. What was a Centurion?

A. An officer in the Roman Army equal in rank to a captain in ours.
2. Q. Where was this Centurion stationed?
A. At Capernaum, on the sea-coast, in the borders of Zebulon and Nepthalim.
3. Q. What character does St. Luke give this Centurion?
A. St. Luke vii. 4, 5.
4. Q. What devout Centurion do we read of in the Acts of the Apostles?
A. Acts x. 1.
1. Q. On what ground did Jesus heal the Centurion's servant?
A. Because he had faith that Jesus could heal him.
2. Q. In what way did he show his faith?
A. By saying to Jesus, "Speak the word only, and my servant shall be healed."
3. Q. What did Christ say of the faith which he manifested?
A. St. Matt. viii. 10, last clause.
4. Q. What did our Saviour say to his disciples in reference to the efficacy of faith?
A. St. Luke xvii. 6.
1. Q. What is one of the most important steps toward faith?
A. A meek and humble spirit, ready and willing to believe.
2. Q. How did the Centurion show this humble spirit?

A. By saying to Jesus, "Lord, I am not worthy that thou shouldest come under my roof."

3. Q. What does St. Paul recommend in the Epistle therefore?
A. Rom. xii. 16.

4. Q. What does St. James assure us will be the effect of humility?
A. St. James iv. 10.

1. Q. What was the result of the faith of the Centurion?
A. His servant was made whole from that hour.

2. Q. What is this a proof of?
A. The power of divinity which resided in Christ, so that even at a distance he could work miracles.

3. Q. Where does Jesus affirm that he possesses this divine power?
A. St. Matt. xxviii. 18.

4. Q. How does the Prophet Isaiah express this power which Jesus Christ should possess?
A. Isaiah ix. 7.

1. Q. Will all Gentiles who believe in Christ be accepted by him?
A. Yes; for he came to save all men of every nation.

2. Q. How do we receive our promise of salvation?
A. Through this general reception of all peoples; for we are Gentiles, and can only be made the children of Christ's kingdom by this acceptance of the Gentiles by Christ.

THIRD SUNDAY AFTER THE EPIPHANY. 51

3. Q. Where is it foretold that the kingdom of Christ should be universal?
A. Dan. vii. 14.
4. Q. How has our Saviour, in a parable, declared that the advantage of being a Jew, or indeed any other privileges, cannot secure heaven to us?
A. St. Luke xiii. 26, 27.
1. Q. Upon what must we depend for strength to gain these promises?
A. As the Collect expresses it, on the right hand of God.
2. Q. What do you mean by the right hand of God?
A. His power and strength, by which he defends us in all our dangers and necessities.
3. Q. How do you know that God will extend this assistance?
A. Psalm xxxiv. 17.
4. Q. What have we to rely upon in praying to God for this assistance besides our own petitions?
A. 1 John ii. 1.

"By faith a steady course we steer,
Through ruffling storms and swelling seas,
O'ercome the world, keep down our fear,
And still possess our souls in peace.

By faith we pass the vale of tears
Safe and serene, though oft distress'd;
By faith subdue the king of fears,
And go rejoicing to our rest."

Hy. 140.

THE FOURTH SUNDAY AFTER THE EPIPHANY.

The Collect.

O GOD, who knowest us to be set in the midst of so many and great dangers, that by reason of the frailty of our nature we cannot always stand upright: Grant to us such strength and protection, as may support us in all dangers, and carry us through all temptations; through Jesus Christ our Lord. Amen.

The Epistle. Rom. xiii. 1.—*The Gospel.* St Matt. viii. 23.

1. Q. What new Epiphany is revealed in the services of to-day?
   A. Christ's power over nature and evil spirits.
2. Q. In what manner is our Saviour made manifest in our day?
   A. By the Bible and blessed sacraments which come through the Church.
3. Q. How are we to continue this manifestation?
   A. St. Matt. x. 27.
4. Q. How universal is the invitation to behold and accept the glory of Christ?
   A. Rev. xxii. 17.
1. Q. How did Jesus manifest his power over nature?
   A. By stilling the tempest.
2. Q. How was this effected?
   A. By saying to the winds and waves, "Peace, be still."
3. Q. What did those who witnessed this miracle say?
   A. St. Matt. viii. 27.

FOURTH SUNDAY AFTER THE EPIPHANY. 53

4. Q. What exclamation of the Psalmist answers to this, as an acknowledgment of the divine power of our Lord?
A. Psa. lxxxix. 8, 9.
1. Q. What rebuke did our Saviour give to his disciples when they awoke him to calm the tempest?
A. That they should have had so little faith.
2. Q. Why did he so rebuke them, when they only yielded to their fears?
A. Because he had been teaching them that faith in him would preserve them, and this conduct showed that they yet doubted.
3. Q. Give another prominent instance of the doubting of one of the disciples?
A. St. John xx. 25.
4. Q. What did our Saviour say of those who, not seeing him, yet believed?
A. St. John xx. 29.
1. Q. How was the power of Christ manifested over evil spirits?
A. By casting out the devils from those who were possessed.
2. Q. Did the unclean spirits recognize Jesus and his power?
A. Yes; for they immediately began to question him, and afterwards obeyed him.
3. Q. What question did they ask him?
A. St. Matt. viii. 29.
4. Q. To what did they refer when they asked him if he came to torment them before the time?

A. Jude 6.

1. Q. How did this miracle differ from the other miracles of our Lord?
A. In that it involved the destruction of the swine, the property of others?

2. Q. Does not this seem to be unjust on the part of Christ?
A. At first it might; but the swine were there contrary to law, and their destruction was only a just punishment for the disobedience of their owners.

3. Q. Where is the law prohibiting the use of swine?
A. Deut. xiv. 8.

4. Q. Where are we told that the devils believe in God?
A. James ii. 19.

1. Q. What did the people desire of Jesus when they saw his works?
A. That he would depart out of their coasts.

2. Q. How is this ingratitude displayed in our day?
A. When we practically send Christ away, by not accepting and believing him.

3. Q. What is the effect of thus sending our Lord away?
A. His glory is hid from us when it would otherwise be manifested.

4. Q. What does St. Paul say will be the effect of the hiding of the gospel from us?
A. 2 Cor. iv. 3.

FOURTH SUNDAY AFTER THE EPIPHANY.

1. Q. What is it that induces men to send Jesus away?
   A. Their love of this world with its pleasures and temptations.
2. Q. Mention some of the greatest temptations which makes Christ distasteful to us?
   A. Riches and honors, pleasures, and even our common employments.
3. Q. What therefore are we warned not to do?
   A. 1 John ii. 15.
4. Q. How does our Saviour put the argument for forsaking the world?
   A. St. Matt. xvi. 26.

1. Q. By whose power can we forsake the world and cleave unto Jesus?
   A. By the power which Jesus gives us.
2. Q. How does this day's lesson show us that Christ's power is sufficient to us?
   A. He, who by the power of his voice could still the tempest and cast out evil spirits, can certainly still the tempest in our souls, and cast out the spirit of evil.
3. Q. What assurance have we that no temptation will be placed in our way which may not be overcome?
   A. 1 Cor. x. 13.
4. Q. What does David say of the faithfulness of the Lord in looking after the interest of his people?
   A. Psa. xxxiii. 18, 19.

"They know the Almighty's power,
 Who, wakened by the rushing midnight shower,
Watch for the fitful breeze
To howl and chafe amid the bending trees,
Watch for the still white gleam
To bathe the landscape in a fiery stream,
Touching the tremulous eye with sense of light
Too rapid and too pure for all but angel sight.

But there are storms within
That heave the struggling heart with wilder din,
And there is power and love
The maniac's rushing frenzy to reprove;
And when he takes his seat,
Cloth'd and in calmness, at his Saviour's feet,
Is not the power as strange, the love as blest,
As when he said, 'Be still,' and ocean sank to rest?"
Keble.

THE FIFTH SUNDAY AFTER THE EPIPHANY.

The Collect.

O LORD, we beseech thee to keep thy Church and household continually in thy true religion; that they who do lean only upon the hope of thy heavenly grace may evermore be defended by thy mighty power; through Jesus Christ our Lord. *Amen.*

The Epistle. Col. iii. 12.—*The Gospel.* St. Matt. xiii. 24.

1. Q. How did our Saviour often illustrate the truth which he taught?
    A. By parables.
2. Q. What is a parable?
    A. A story founded on familiar things, which will show the meaning of the truth illustrated.

3. Q. What did our Saviour answer, when his disciples asked him why he spoke in parables?
A. St. Matt. xiii. 11.
4. Q. How do we know that Jesus did not mean by this, that he did not wish the people to understand his words?
A. 1 Tim. ii. 3, 4.
1. Q. To whom will parables come as lessons full of meaning?
A. To those who are willing to listen and obey.
2. Q. What will parables be to those who are not willing to receive them?
A. They will be "dark sayings, hard to understand."
3. Q. Did the Prophet Isaiah foretell that there should be such people?
A. Isaiah vi. 9.
4. Q. What did our Saviour say to those who believed in his parables?
A. St. Matt. xiii. 16.
1. Q. What is the object of the parable in the gospel for the day?
A. To show how strongly Satan will work against Christ and his kingdom.
2. Q. What is this kingdom of Christ on earth called?
A. The Church, founded on the Apostles and Prophets, Jesus Christ being the chief cornerstone.
3. Q. When is the Church called the body of which Christ is the head?

A. Col. i. 18.
4. Q. What reason have we for believing that Satan will not prevail over the Church?
A. St. Matt. xxviii. 20, last clause.
1. Q. Who is meant by the sower?
A. Christ our blessed Lord.
2. Q. What are the good seed and the tares?
A. "The good seed are the children of the kingdom; but the tares are the children of the wicked one."
3. Q. Who sowed seed after the ascension of Christ?
A. 1 Cor. iii. 6.
4. Q. Were the Gentiles to be included in this field into which the seed was to be sown?
A. St. Mark xvi. 15.
1. Q. Who sowed tares in the field while men slept?
A. The devil, who is Christ's enemy.
2. Q. By what wiles does the devil seek to introduce tares into our hearts?
A. By vain doctrines and evil temptations.
3. Q. What has St. Paul recommended us to do, to resist the wiles of the devil?
A. Eph. vi. 11.
4. Q. Are we anywhere told that our resistance to the devil will accomplish this result?
A. St. James iv. 7.
1. Q. When the tares sprang up, what did the servants say?
A. They asked him if they should root them out.

2. Q. What answer did he give them?
   A. "Let both grow together till the harvest."
3. Q. When will the harvest come and who are the reapers?
   A. St. Matt. xiii. 39.
4. Q. How do we know that the Holy Angels will come with Christ in judgment?
   A. St. Matt. xxv. 31.
1. Q. Who do the wheat and tares represent?
   A. Those who love Christ and those who serve Satan.
2. Q. What shall be done with the tares or the wicked?
   A. They shall be gathered together and cast into the furnace.
3. Q. What will be the lot of the wheat or righteous?
   A. St. Matt. xiii. 43.
4. Q. What shall be the character of the Church at this time?
   A. Eph. v. 27.
1. Q. For what do we pray in the collect?
   A. That God will keep his Church and household continually in his true religion.
2. Q. What do you understand by the word Church?
   A. That society of men, in which the word of God is rightly taught and the sacraments duly administered by properly ordained persons.
3. Q. What does St. Paul tell us to do in order to preserve the Church in unity and purity?
   A. Col. iii. 12.

4. Q. In whose name are we to act and speak, when we would further the interests of Christ's Church?
A. Col. iii. 17.

"O God! by whom the seed is given;
By whom the harvest blest;
Whose word, like manna shower'd from heaven,
Is planted in our breast;

"Preserve it from the passing feet,
And plunderers of the air;
The sultry sun's intenser heat,
And weeds of worldly care!

"Though buried deep, or thinly strewn,
Do thou thy grace supply;
The hope in earthly furrows sown
Shall blossom in the sky."

THE SIXTH SUNDAY AFTER THE EPIPHANY.
The Collect.

O GOD, whose blessed Son was manifested that he might destroy the works of the devil, and make us the sons of God, and heirs of eternal life; Grant us, we beseech thee, that, having this hope, we may purify ourselves, even as he is pure; that, when he shall appear again with power and great glory, we may be made like unto him in his eternal and glorious kingdom; where with thee, O Father, and thee, O Holy Ghost, he liveth and reigneth, ever one God, world without end. *Amen.*

The Epistle. 1 St. John iii. 1.—*The Gospel.* St. Matt. xxiv. 23.

1. Q. What grand Epiphany is referred to in the gospel of the day?

SIXTH SUNDAY AFTER THE EPIPHANY.

 A. Christ's manifestation in the clouds with power and great glory.

2. Q. When will this manifestation of Christ occur?
 A. At the end of the world.
3. Q. What answer did Christ make when his disciples asked him of the signs of his coming?
 A. St. Matt. xxiv. 15.
4. Q. To what prophecy does St. Matthew refer?
 A. Dan. ix. 27—xii. ii.

1. Q. What did our Saviour say should be one of the first signs?
 A. False Christs and false prophets should arise.
2. Q. Is there any evidence that such really did arise?
 A. History mentions quite a number who led many to destruction.
3. Q. Were there any such impostors who had already appeared?
 A. Acts v. 36, 37.
4. Q. What similar testimony is found in the prophecy of Jeremiah?
 A. Jer. xiv. 14.

1. Q. What should these false Christs and prophets endeavor to do?
 A. To deceive if possible even the elect.
2. Q. Who are the elect?
 A. The sons of God, who have become his children through the love of Christ.
3. Q. How do we know that these impostors shall not succeed in their object?
 A. St. John x. 28.

4. Q. What is St. Paul's opinion of the ability of Christ to fulfil this promise?
A. Heb. vii. 25.
1. Q. How is the coming of "the Son of man" described?
A. As the lightning coming out of the East.
2. Q. What is this expression designed to represent?
A. The suddenness and rapidity of the coming of Christ.
3. Q. Where does Christ acknowledge his name of "the Son of man"?
A. St. Matt. xvi. 13.
4. Q. What caution does our Saviour suggest on account of the suddenness of his coming?
A. St. Matt. xxiv. 42.
1. Q. What else does our Saviour suggest in this place?
A. The surety of the judgment.
2. Q. In what figure is this truth expressed?
A. "Wheresoever the carcass is, there will the eagles be gathered together."
3. Q. How does this express the certainty of the judgment?
A. "As the carcass everywhere attracts the carrion-eaters, so do moral corruption and ripened guilt everywhere demand the judgment."
4. Q. Where is this figure used to describe the manner of the destruction of Jerusalem?
A. Habak. i. 8.
1. Q. What other signs shall announce the coming of Christ?

SIXTH SUNDAY AFTER THE EPIPHANY.

    A. The sun and moon shall be darkened, and the stars shall fall.
2. Q. What do these figures denote in Scripture?
    A. The great calamities which befall kings and nations.
3. Q. Give an example when these signs attended these calamities.
    A. Ezek. xxxii. 7. Joel iii. 15.
4. Q. What further signs are found in St. Luke's account?
    A. St. Luke xxi. 25, 26.
1. Q. What shall then appear?
    A. "The Son of man" in the heavens.
2. Q. What effect will it have upon the tribes of the earth?
    A. They shall mourn and tremble.
3. Q. Why will they mourn at his presence then?
    A. Rev. i. 7.
4. Q. How did Christ ascend into heaven?
    A. Acts i. 9.
1. Q. Whom will he send?
    A. An angel or messenger.
2. Q. What will the angel do?
    A. Gather together those who are chosen of God, from the four winds of heaven.
3. Q. What does St. John say shall be our condition when He appears, if we love him?
    A. 1 St. John iii. 2.
4. Q. What is the object of the first as well as the last Epiphany?

A. 1 John iii. 8, last clause.

> ' What is the heaven our God bestows
> No prophet yet, no angel knows;
> Was never yet created eye
> Could see across eternity;
> Not seraphs' wings forever soaring
> Can pass the flight of souls adoring,
> That nearer still and nearer grow
> To th' unapproached Lord, once made for them so low."
> *Keble.*

SEPTUAGESIMA SUNDAY.

The Collect.

O LORD, we beseech thee favourably to hear the prayers of thy people, that we, who are justly punished for our offences, may be mercifully delivered by thy goodness, for the glory of thy name, through JESUS CHRIST our Saviour, who liveth and reigneth with thee and the HOLY GHOST, ever one GOD, world without end. *Amen.*

The Epistle. 1. Cor. ix. 24.—*The Gospel.* St. Matt. xx. 1.

1. Q. Why is this Sunday called Septuagesima?
   A. Because it is about seventy days before Easter.
2. Q. What is this season designed to teach us?
   A. To draw our minds from the joyful thoughts of Christmas to consider the humiliation of our Lord, during Lent.
3. Q. What is promised to the humble who seek to improve such seasons as these?
   A. Ps. x. 17.

SEPTUAGESIMA SUNDAY.

4. Q. What kind of preparation does St. Paul suggest?
A. Eph. vi. 15.
1. Q. What is the intention of the Epistle and Gospel for the day?
A. To show us that our bodies as well as our spirits must be kept in subjection, so that we may do the work of our Lord.
2. Q. How does our Saviour illustrate this truth?
A. By showing us in this parable what the kingdom of heaven is like.
3. Q. How does St. Matthew describe the construction of a vineyard?
A. St. Matt. xxi. 33.
4. Q. What did Isaiah say the vineyard of the Lord was?
A. Isai. v. 7.
1. Q. What did the owner of the vineyard do?
A. He went out to hire labourers.
2. Q. What wages did he offer the men whom he employed?
A. A penny a day—equal in value to about 14 cents of our money.
3. Q. Does Christ demand that we should work for him?
A. St. Matt. vii. 21.
4. Q. What is the difference between the wages of Christ and those of Sin?
A. Rom. vi. 23.
1. Q. What did the master say to those whom he found idle at the third hour?

SEPTUAGESIMA SUNDAY.

A. "Go ye also into the vineyard, and whatsoever is right I will give you.
2. Q. Did he go out again?
A. At the sixth and ninth hour he went out and did likewise.
3. Q. Does God particularly call the young to his service?
A. Eccles. xii. 1.
4. Q. Will industry benefit a man in the eyes of God unless he works in his vineyard?
A. St. Mark viii 36.
1. Q. What did the master do at the Eleventh hour?
A. Finding others standing idle he set them to work.
2. Q. Did he promise these men any reward?
A. "Whatsoever is right that shall ye receive."
3. Q. Are we commanded not to be idle?
A. Phil. ii. 12.
4. Q. What reason have we for believing that we must enter upon our work, even though we be near unto death?
A. Eccles. ix. 10.
1. Q. What did the Lord command at even?
A. That the labourers should be paid their wages.
2. Q. Who will give us our reward?
A. Christ himself, at the final day when we are judged.
3. Q. How shall our works be made manifest on that day?
A. 1 Cor. iii. 13.

SEPTUAGESIMA SUNDAY. 67

4. Q. What shall be this reward for the labours of a faithful life in Christ's vineyard?
   A. Rom. ii. 7.
1. Q. How much did those who were hired last receive?
   A. As much as those who were first employed.
2. Q. What example have we in the gospel of the call and reward of one, who began to serve Christ at the Eleventh hour?
   A. The penitent thief who suffered for his crime; when our Saviour was crucified.
3. Q. To what among other things does this parable refer?
   A. To the calling of the Gentiles at a later age of the world?
4. Q. Of what nation shall the blessed multitude in heaven be composed?
   A. Rev. vii. 9.
1. Q. Who are "called" in the gospel?
   A. All who hear the word of Christ.
2. Q. What is it that hinders us from accepting this call?
   A. Nothing but our own stubborn and unwilling hearts.
3. Q. What does Christ require of us in order to gain admission into his vineyard?
   A. St. Luke xiii. 24.
4. Q. What assures us that the joys of heaven are worth the labour of our lives?
   A. 1 Cor. ii. 9.

"Two worlds are ours; 'tis only sin
  Forbid us to descry
The mystic heaven and earth within,
  Plain as the sea and sky.

Thou, who hast given me eyes to see
  And love this sight so fair,
Give me a heart to find out Thee,
  And read Thee everywhere."

Keble.

SEXAGESIMA SUNDAY.

The Collect.

O LORD God, who seest that we put not our trust in any thing that we do; Mercifully grant that by thy power we may be defended against all adversity; through Jesus Christ our Lord. Amen.

The Epistle. 2 Cor. xi. 19.—*The Gospel.* St. Luke viii. 4.

1. Q. What does the Epistle for this day teach?
   A. To keep our bodies in subjection.
2. Q. What was the object of St. Paul in mortifying his body?
   A. That his Soul might be free to receive the truth and do it.
3. Q. What confession of St. Paul shows the necessity and wisdom of this mortification?
   A. Rom. vii. 23.
4. Q. Are we required to serve God with our *bodies* as well as our spirits?
   A. Rom. xii. i. 1 Cor. vi. 20.
1. Q. What is the object of the gospel for the day?

SEXAGESIMA SUNDAY.

    A. To teach us how to hear the truth.
2. Q. What is the way to hear the truth of Christ aright?
    A. By diligent study and willingness to be instructed.
3. Q. How did Jeremiah express this same truth to the Jews?
    A. Jer. iv. 3.
4. Q. What does our Saviour say of those who hear the truth but do not seek to apply it?
    A. St. Matt. xiii. 14.
1. Q. How did Christ teach this truth to the multitude about him?
    A. By the parable of the Sower.
2. Q. What do you mean by a parable?
    A. An illustration taken from earthly objects, to instruct us in heavenly truths.
3. Q. Was our Saviour in the habit of speaking in parables?
    A. St. Matt. xiii. 34.
4. Q. What prophecy did he thus fulfil?
    A. Ps. lxxviii. 2.
1. Q. What did the Sower do?
    A. He went out into his field to sow seed.
2. Q. What does the seed represent?
    A. The word of God which is sown by his ministers.
3. Q. What does St. Peter say of the word of God?
    A. 1 St. Peter i. 25.
4. Q. To whom is the word of God sent?

A. Acts xiii. 26.
1. Q. Where did our Saviour say the seed fell?
   A. Some by the wayside, where it was trodden down.
2. Q. Who are represented by the seed that fell on the wayside.
   A. Those who hear carelessly and allow the devil to take the word away from their hearts.
3. Q. How can we prevent the devil from taking away the word?
   A. St. James iv. 7.
4. Q. How may we always keep the word which is preached constantly before us?
   A. St. John v. 39.
1. Q. Where else did the seed fall?
   A. On a rock, where it soon withered, because it had no moisture to sustain it.
2. Q. What does our Saviour compare this seed to?
   A. To those who hear the word joyfully, but in temptation fall away again.
3. Q. Does God tempt any man to sin?
   A. St. James i. 13.
4. Q. What encouragement have we in the hour of temptation if we really seek to avoid it?
   A. 1 Cor. x. 13.
1. Q. Some of the seed fell among thorns, why did not this grow up and flourish?
   A. Because the thorns, like weeds in a garden, overran the tender plants.
2. Q. What prevents the word from bearing good fruit in some who hear it?

 A. The cares, riches and pleasures of this world, which take away the strength from the tender shoots of righteousness.
8. Q. What is said of those who are absorbed in their love for the things of this world?
 A. 1 St. John ii. 15.
4. Q. What is the danger in the future to those who are described as being cursed by the cares and riches of this world?
 A. Heb. vi. 8.
1. Q. What became of the seed that fell upon the good ground?
 A. It sprang up and bore a great abundance of fruit.
2. Q. In whom does the word of God produce good fruit?
 A. In those who patiently receiving the word into honest and good hearts, endeavour to cultivate it by every means which the grace of God has given them.
3. Q. How are we enabled to bring our fruit to perfection?
 A. St. John xv. 5.
4. Q. What is the great reason why we should strive to bear fruit?
 A. St. John xv. 8.

  If niggard earth her treasures hide,
   To all but labouring hands denied,
  Lavish of thorns and worthless weeds alone,

The doom is half in mercy given,
　To train us in our way to heaven,
And shew our lagging souls how glory must be won.

　　If on the sinner's outward frame
　　God hath impress'd His mark of blame,
And even our bodies shrink at touch of light,
　　Yet mercy hath not left us bare;
　　The very weeds we daily wear
Are to Faith's eye a pledge of God's forgiving might.

QUINQUAGESIMA SUNDAY.

The Collect.

O LORD, who hast taught us that all our doings without charity are nothing worth; Send Thy Holy Ghost, and pour into our hearts that most excellent gift of charity, the very bond of peace and of all virtues, without which whosoever liveth is counted dead before thee. Grant this for thine only Son Jesus Christ's sake. *Amen.*

The Epistle. 1 Cor. xiii. 1.—*The Gospel.* St. Luke xviii. 31.

1. Q. What are we taught to-day in preparation for Lent?
   A. That our humility, with all other acts of devotion, must spring from charity.
2. Q. What is the meaning of charity in this connection?
   A. Love to God and our neighbors.
3. Q. What does St. Paul say of the necessity of charity?
   A. 1 Cor. xiii. 1.

4. Q. What two laws did our Saviour give in reference to charity?
A. St. Matt. xxii. 37–39.
1. Q. What are our good actions worth without charity?
A. They are good for nothing.
2. Q. Will God accept our best services unaccompanied by charity?
A. No! for he has taught us that our good deeds must be the result of our love for him.
3. Q. How do we know that our love for God will make us acceptable to him?
A. 1 Cor. viii. 3.
4. Q. Can a man love God and at the same time hate his brother?
A. 1 John iv. 20.
1. Q. What is charity called in the collect for to-day?
A. "The very bond of peace and of all virtues."
2. Q. How is charity so powerful in its effects?
A. Because it prevents dissension among Christians and fills them with a desire for the good of others.
3. Q. What does St. Paul tell the Romans is their duty to their Christian brethren?
A. Rom. xii. 10.
4. Q. What does our Saviour say will be the effect of brotherly love?
A. St. John xiii. 35.
1. Q. How does the collect say we shall be esteemed if we have not charity?

A. We shall be "counted dead" before God.
2. Q. What does this mean?
A. That whosoever lives without charity shall die the second death, without any hope of life everlasting.
3. Q. What does St. John say of those who do not love God?
A. 1 John iv. 8.
4. Q. What scripture evidence have we that he that hateth his brother has no hope of everlasting life?
A. 1 St. John iii. 15.
1. Q. How did our Saviour show his charity at this time?
A. By restoring the sight of the blind man at Jericho.
2. Q. How did the blind man make his appeal for Christ's assistance?
A. "Jesus, thou son of David, have mercy on me."
3. Q. What was his authority for calling Jesus "the son of David?"
A. St. Matt. xxii. 42.
4. Q. Is Christ represented as being peculiarly merciful and loving?
A. Eph. iii. 18, 19.
1. Q. What lack of charity did the disciples show to this poor blind man?
A. When they heard him calling on Jesus, they rebuked him.
2. Q. What did the blind man do when he was told to hold his peace?

3. Q. Are all, like the blind, in darkness, who are without the gospel?
A. Acts xxvi. 17, 18.
4. Q. How is it possible for us to be cured of our spiritual blindness?
A. St. John viii. 12.

"Lord, with glowing heart I'd praise thee
For the bliss thy love bestows;
For the pard'ning grace that saves me,
And the peace that from it flows:
Help, O God, my weak endeavour;
This dull soul to rapture raise:
Thou must light the flame, or never
Can my love be warm'd to praise."

Hy. 150.

ASH WEDNESDAY.

The Collect.

ALMIGHTY and everlasting God, who hatest nothing that thou hast made, and dost forgive the sins of all those who are penitent; Create and make in us new and contrite hearts, that we worthily lamenting our sins, and acknowledging our wretchedness, may obtain of thee, the God of all mercy, perfect remission and forgiveness; through Jesus Christ our Lord.
Amen.

At Morning Prayer, the Litany being ended, shall be said the following Prayers, immediately before the General Thanksgiving.

O LORD, we beseech thee, mercifully hear our prayers, and spare all those who confess their sins unto

A. He cried out more earnestly than ever.
3. Q. Are we exhorted to like earnestness in our prayers for mercy?
A. St. Luke xviii. 1.
4. Q. What did our Saviour say of importunity in prayer, in his parable immediately after teaching his disciples the Lord's Prayer?
A. St. Luke xi. 8.
1. Q. What did our Saviour ask of the blind man?
A. Why he had called upon him and what he wanted.
2. Q. What was his reply?
A. "And he said, Lord, that I may receive my sight."
3. Q. Was this a very great request which the poor man asked of Jesus?
A. St. John ix. 32.
4. Q. Does Christ give us the liberty of applying for his mercy in all our necessities?
A. St. John xiv. 13, 14.
1. Q. What did Jesus require in this man which he also demands of us before he grants our requests?
A. Faith in him, that he can do what we desire of him.
2. Q. What did the blind man do after he had received his sight, which we should strive to copy?
A. He followed Christ, as we should devote ourselves to him for his many mercies to us.

thee; that they, whose consciences by sin are accused, by thy merciful pardon may be absolved; through Christ our Lord. *Amen.*

O MOST mighty God, and merciful Father, who hast compassion upon all men, and hatest nothing that thou hast made; who wouldest not the death of a sinner, but rather that he should turn from his sin, and be saved; Mercifully forgive us our trespasses; receive and comfort us, who are grieved and wearied with the burden of our sins. Thy property is always to have mercy; to thee only it appertaineth to forgive sins. Spare us therefore, good Lord, spare thy people, whom thou hast redeemed; enter not into judgment with thy servants, who are vile earth, and miserable sinners; but so turn thine anger from us, who meekly acknowledge our vileness, and truly repent us of our faults, and so make haste to help us in this world, that we may ever live with thee in the world to come; through Jesus Christ our Lord. *Amen.*

Then shall the people say this that followeth, after the Minister.

TURN thou us, O good Lord, and so shall we be turned. Be favourable, O Lord, Be favourable to thy people, Who turn to thee in weeping, fasting, and praying. For thou art a merciful God, Full of compassion, Long-suffering, and of great pity. Thou sparest when we deserve punishment, And in thy wrath thinkest upon mercy. Spare thy people, good Lord, spare them, And let not thine heritage be brought to confusion. Hear us, O Lord, for thy mercy is great, And after the multitude of thy mercies look upon us; Through the merits and mediation of thy blessed Son, Jesus Christ our Lord. AMEN.

For the Epistle. Joel ii. 12.—*The Gospel.* St. Matt. vi. 16.

1. Q. What is the meaning of the word Lent?

ASH WEDNESDAY.

    A. Spring, and is applied to the spring fast of 40 days.

2. Q. In remembrance of what do we keep the fast of Lent?

    A. In remembrance of the forty days fast in the wilderness by our Saviour.

3. Q. How should we keep this fast?

    A. By abstaining from unnecessary indulgences and devoting our thoughts to humility and prayer.

4. Q. Give an example from the Old Testament of a fast of forty days?

    A. Exod. xxxiv. 28.   1 Kings xix. 8.

1. Q. What is the first day of Lent commonly called?

    A. Ash Wednesday.

2. Q. From what custom is this name derived?

    A. From the primitive custom of sprinkling ashes on the heads of penitents on this day.

3. Q. Give an instance of this custom as recorded in Daniel?

    A. Dan. ix. 3.

4. Q. What did our Saviour say of Tyre and Sidon in connection with this custom?

    A. St. Matt. xi. 21.

1. Q. Why does Ash Wednesday come forty-six days before Easter?

    A. Because the six Sundays in Lent are taken out, leaving only forty days of fasting.

2. Q. Why are the Sundays not regarded as fast days?

A. Because, Sunday being the day on which we celebrate the Lord's resurrection, it has always been regarded as a feast and day of joy.

8. Q. What was generally done to those who were convicted of notorious crimes, on Ash Wednesday?
A. They were put to open penance and excommunicated by the Bishop.

4. Q. When they repented, how were they re-admitted into the Church?
A. By absolution, from the Bishop or Priest who, persuaded of their penitence, restored them to the communion.

1. Q. What is the chief object of the Lenten season?
A. To lead us to repentance.

2. Q. What is the nature of true repentance?
A. Hearty sorrow for sins past, with sincere resolutions, by the grace of God, to forsake them.

3. Q. What therefore are we called upon to do in the Epistle?
A. Joel ii. 13.

4. Q. How are we instructed to fast in the gospel?
A. St. Matt. vi. 17, 18.

1. Q. Why should we be sorry for our sins?
A. Because sin grieves God, and causes him to draw his favour from us.

2. Q. What should incite us to repentance?
A. Our gratitude to God, who has graciously provided a way of escape from the evils of sin, for those who repent and believe in his Son.

ASH WEDNESDAY.

3. Q. Where do we read that God is grieved at the wicked?
A. Psalm vii. 11.
4. Q. What will be our condition if we neglect repentance?
A. St. Luke xiii. 3.
1. Q. How should we express our sorrow for sin?
A. By confession, by fasting and humbly asking pardon for Christ's sake.
2. Q. Upon what should our sorrow for sin be founded?
A. On our appreciation of the vileness of sin, and the need of God's grace to overcome it.
3. Q. What example have we, in the acts of the Holy Apostles, of fasting for sin?
A. Acts ix. 9.
4. Q. Are reparation and restitution necessary fruits of true repentance?
A. Levit. vi. 4, 5.
1. Q. In what consists the necessity of repentance?
A. It is necessary to salvation.
2. Q. Is repentance, then, the cause of our salvation?
A. No; Jesus Christ by his atonement purchased our salvation, but remission of sin is nevertheless dependent on our penitence.
3. Q. What does St. Peter say is essential for the remission of sins?
A. Acts ii. 38.
4. Q. What is said of the joy in heaven over the penitent sinner?

A. St. Luke xv. 7.
1. Q. When should we begin our repentance?
A. To-day, for we know not how long a time we have in which to repent.
2. Q. Is it possible to repent on the death-bed?
A. Yes, but it is dangerous to neglect it till then.
3. Q. What reason does our Saviour give why we should repent at once?
A. St. Luke xii. 40.
4. Q. What reason does the Preacher give, why children should repent while they are young?
A. Eccles. xii. 1.

"Oh let us keep our fast within,
Till heaven and we are quite alone,
Then let the grief, the shame, the sin,
Before the mercy-seat be thrown.
Between the porch and altar weep,
Unworthy of the holiest place,
Yet hoping near the shrine to keep
Our lowly cell in sight of grace."
Keble.

THE FIRST SUNDAY IN LENT.

The Collect.

O LORD, who for our sake didst fast forty days and forty nights; Give us grace to use such abstinence, that, our flesh being subdued to the Spirit, we may ever obey thy godly motions in righteousness, and true holiness, to thy honour and glory, who livest and reignest with the Father and the Holy Ghost, one God, world without end. *Amen.*

THE FIRST SUNDAY IN LENT.

The Epistle. 2 Cor. vi. 1.—*The Gospel.* St. Matt. iv. 1.

1. Q. Are the Sundays in Lent fast days?
   A. No, but they partake of the solemn nature of the season.
2. Q. Why are these Sundays observed as feasts?
   A. Because they commemorate the resurrection of Christ and are therefore joyous in their character.
3. Q. What confirmation have we of the joyous nature of Sunday?
   A. Ps. cxviii. 24.
4. Q. Give an instance when the first day of the week was celebrated as the day of rest and worship, instead of the Jewish Sabbath?
   A. Acts xx. 7.
1. Q. In what are we instructed this day?
   A. Of the necessity of fasting.
2. Q. What do we mean by fasting?
   A. Denying our appetites and abstaining from worldy indulgences.
3. Q. What example of fasting is given us in the gospel?
   A. St. Matt. iv. 1, 2.
4. Q. What does St. Peter tell us we should do in our warfare against evil?
   A. 1 St. Peter ii. 11.
1. Q. Before what event did our Saviour fast forty days and forty nights?
   A. Before his temptation in the wilderness.

Q. Why did Jesus, who was sinless, fast in preparation for his temptation?
A. In order that we might have a perfect example, in our efforts in overcoming sin.
Q. In the Epistle, what is included in those things by which we "approve ourselves" as ministers of God.
A. 2 Cor. vi. 5.
Q. Did our Saviour attach any reward to fasting?
A. St. Matt. vi. 18.
Q. What is the object of fasting?
A. That our flesh may be subject to our spirit.
Q. What do you mean by this?
A. That by conquering the desires of our flesh, we may more easily obey the commands of the spirit.
Q. How did St. Paul express this war of the spiritual and carnal nature within him?
A. Rom. vii. 23.
Q. What conclusion does he draw from this natural condition?
A. Rom. viii. 13.
Q. What may we learn from the temptation of Christ?
A. That the devil will tempt even the holiest person.
Q. What is shown in the method of his temptation?
A. His power in suiting his temptations to the condition of those whom he desires to destroy.
Q. What does St. Peter recommend on account of the vigilance of the devil?

A. 1 St. Peter v. 8.
4. Q. Does St. James encourage us that if we follow the example of Christ we shall conquer?
A. St. James iv. 7.
1. Q. How did our Saviour overcome Satan?
A. By answering him, "it is written."
2. Q. How should we endeavour to overcome his temptations?
A. By a strict adherence to the commands "which are written."
3. Q. What is said of him that overcometh unto the end?
A. Rev. ii. 11.
4. Q. How are we told to overcome evil?
A. Rom. xii. 21.
1. Q. What happened after the temptation of Christ?
A. Angels came and ministered to him.
2. Q. What comfort do we gather from this?
A. That if we resist temptation, we also shall receive comfort.
3. Q. Will God relieve us in all our temptations?
A. 1 Cor. x. 13.
4. Q. How can we obtain his assistance?
A. Heb. iv. 16.
1. Q. What season is this day also the beginning of?
A. The Lenten Ember season.
2. Q. What are Ember days?
A. Days set apart at the four seasons, to invoke the divine aid in the choice of ministers of the gospel.

THE SECOND SUNDAY IN LENT.

3. Q. When do these days come?
   A. On the Wednesdays, Fridays, and Saturdays after the first Sunday in Lent, after Whitsunday, and after the 14th of September and the 13th of December.
4. Q. What scripture authority have we for this observance?
   A. Acts xiv. 23.

"O Lord, the wilderness to me
A very paradise shall be,
Since Thou for forty days wast there,
In fasting, solitude, and prayer.

Unworthy though these feet to rest
On ground Thy footsteps once have blest,
Thy way of sorrows shall be mine,
Made sweet because it first was thine.

Some quiet aisle, or dim recess,
Shall make for me a wilderness;
And surely angels shall be there
To wait on penitence and prayer."

THE SECOND SUNDAY IN LENT.

The Collect.

ALMIGHTY God, who seest that we have no power of ourselves to help ourselves; keep us both outwardly in our bodies, and inwardly in our souls; that we may be defended from all adversities which may happen to the body, and from all evil thoughts which may assault and hurt the soul, through JESUS CHRIST our Lord. *Amen.*

THE SECOND SUNDAY IN LENT.

The Epistle. 1 Thess. iv. 1.—*The Gospel.* St. Matt. xv. 21.

1. Q. What do we learn in the service of to-day?
   A. Our inclination to Sin and the disposition of Christ to forgive.
2. Q. Have we the power to resist this inclination to do evil?
   A. "We have no power of ourselves to help ourselves."
3. Q. Where else are we instructed of our insufficiency?
   A. 2 Cor. iii. 5.
4. Q. Does St. Peter assure us of the support of God?
   A. 1 Peter i. 5.

1. Q. What do you mean by our insufficiency in helping ourselves?
   A. That we cannot keep our bodies from harm or our souls from sin.
2. Q. To whom then must we look for help?
   A. Unto God, through the mercy of Christ our Saviour?
3. Q. Is God able to help us?
   A. St. Jude 24.
4. Q. What does David say of the power of God in our troubles?
   A. Ps. xlvi. 1.

1. Q. What is it that assaults our souls?
   A. Evil thoughts and vain imaginations.
2. Q. How do evil thoughts assault the soul?
   A. By tempting it, and drawing it into sin; thereby defiling it.

THE SECOND SUNDAY IN LENT.   87

3. Q. Are the imaginations of the heart naturally evil?
   A. Gen. vi. 5.
4. Q. What encouragement is held out for us to turn to God in the time of temptation?
   A. Isai. lv. 7.
1. Q. What evidence have we in the gospel for to-day of the willingness of Christ to help us?
   A. That he listened to the cry of the woman of Canaan.
2. Q. Did Christ listen to her immediately?
   A. No, he waited to try her faith.
3. Q. What did the disciples urge him to do?
   A. St. Matt. xv. 23.
4. Q. How does his answer show that he will hear all who ask him?
   A. St. Matt. xv. 24.
1. Q. Why was the helping of this woman of Canaan a peculiar evidence of Christ's mercy?
   A. Because she was not a Jew but one of the Gentile race.
2. Q. Was this fact against her?
   A. Yes, because her race had been doomed to total extinction by the curse of God.
3. Q. How then, in accordance with the promise of God to Abraham, could this woman receive a blessing from our Saviour?
   A. Gen. xxii. 18.
4. Q. Did Christ acknowledge that there was hope for others besides the Jews?
   A. St. John x. 16.

1. Q. What answer did the woman make when Jesus said that it was "not meet to take the children's bread and cast it unto dogs?"
   A. "Truth, Lord, yet the dogs eat of the crumbs which fall from their master's table."
2. Q. What did she mean by this?
   A. That though she was not worthy to receive the best, yet she desired a little of his mercy.
3. Q. Are any of us worthy of the favour of Christ?
   A. Rom. iii. 12.
4. Q. How did Jacob express his sense of unworthiness?
   A. Gen. xxxii. 10, first clause.
1. Q. Did the woman of Canaan receive an answer to her prayer?
   A. "Her daughter was made whole from that hour."
2. Q. On what ground did she receive it?
   A. Because of her faith and earnestness in asking.
3. Q. Will God exorcise the demon of sin within us if we repent and ask his assistance?
   A. Dan. ix. 9, 10.
4. Q. What then is your duty in order to obtain the forgiveness of God?
   A. St. Luke xv. 18, 19.
1. Q. What does the example of this woman teach us?
   A. To "continue constant in prayer."
2. Q. How are we encouraged by her final success?
   A. That though God may for a time hide his face from us, yet he will finally hear us if we persevere in our prayer.

3. Q. How often should we pray for forgiveness?
A. St. Luke xviii. 1.
4. Q. What does St. Paul say to the Galatians in reference to perseverance in well doing?
A. Gal. vi. 9.

" And is there in God's world so drear a place
   Where the loud bitter cry is raised in vain?
Where tears of penance come too late for grace,
   As on the uprooted flowers the genial rain?

'Tis even so: the Sovereign Lord of souls
   Stores in the dungeon of his boundless realm
Each bolt, that o'er the sinner vainly rolls,
   With gathered wrath the reprobate to whelm."
Keble.

THE THIRD SUNDAY IN LENT.

The Collect.

WE beseech thee, Almighty God, look upon the hearty desires of thy humble servants, and stretch forth the right hand of thy Majesty, to be our defence against all our enemies; through Jesus Christ our Lord. *Amen.*

The Epistle. Eph. v. 1.—*The Gospel.* St. Luke xi. 14.

1. Q. Of what are we reminded in the services of to-day?
A. The power of Satan and his angels.
2. Q. What power has Satan and his angels over men?
A. The power of leading them into temptation.

3. Q. What instance can you relate of the presumption of the devil in tempting our Saviour?
A. St. Mark i. 13.
4. Q. What is the testimony of St. Peter of the power of Satan?
A. 1 St. Peter v. 8.
1. Q. What power is revealed which is capable of destroying the power of Satan?
A. The power of Jesus Christ.
2. Q. What is this power called in the Collect, which used to be applied to Christ?
A. "The right hand of God's majesty."
3. Q. How did Christ show this power over Satan when he was tempted?
A. St. Matt. iv. 10.
4. Q Does this give us confidence that he can help us when we are tempted?
A. Heb. ii. 18.
1. Q. How was this power of Christ manifested in the gospel for to-day.
A. By his casting out a devil from the dumb man.
2. Q. What was the cause of the deafness and dumbness of this afflicted man?
A. The demon which was in him.
3. Q. Why do you think it was through the influence of the demon?
A. St. Luke xi. 14.
4. Q. Does Satan close the senses of those whom he would destroy?
A. St. Matt. xiii. 15.

THE THIRD SUNDAY IN LENT.

1. Q. By what power did the unbelieving people say that our Saviour cast out the devil?
   A. "Through Beelzebub, the chief of the devils."
2. Q. What was the object of the Pharisees in this accusation?
   A. That the people might not believe in the power of Christ to work miracles.
3. Q. Were miracles designed to show forth Christ's power and glory?
   A. St John ii. 11.
4. Q. From what words of St. Peter do we gather the idea that on the miracles was founded a proof of Christ's power?
   A. 2 St. Peter i. 16.

1. Q. How did our Saviour answer this charge of the Pharisees?
   A. "If Satan be divided against himself how shall his kingdom stand?"
2. Q. What did our Saviour mean by asking them "By whom do your sons cast them out?"
   A. To rebuke those who believed that their sons who were exorcists had power over devils.
3. Q. How do we know that the cures of the exorcists were incomplete.
   A. St. Matt. ix. 33.
4. Q. In what other place in Scripture is this power called "the finger of God."
   A. Ex. viii. 19.

1. Q. Of what did Christ say that this miracle was an evidence?

    A. That the kingdom of God had come among them.
2. Q. What did he mean by this?
    A. That He, by this, proved his divinity, and therefore the truth of his mission.
3. Q. In what does St. Paul say, consists the kingdom of God?
    A. 1 Cor. iv. 20.
4. Q. What is the kingdom of God, or the Church of Christ called in the Colossians?
    A. Col. i. 24.
1. Q. Of what does the gospel warn us?
    A. To watch against the attacks of the devil.
2. Q. How can we do this?
    A. By constantly examining our hearts, and asking God to search our hearts.
3. Q. How did David ask God to assist him in this duty?
    A. Ps. cxxxix. 23, 24.
4. Q. What greatest of all sins did our Saviour warn the Pharisees of at the time that he worked this miracle?
    A. St. Matt. xii. 31.
1. Q. How did Jesus conclude this miracle?
    A. By the promise of a blessing to those who are faithful.
2. Q. Do we learn any thing from the manner in which he said this?
    A. Yes; that though his Holy mother was blessed among women, yet more blessed was he that believed.

3. Q. In what then consisted the greatest honour of the Blessed Virgin?,

A. That she was united to him not only as his mother but as her Saviour and Redeemer.

4. Q. How can we gather from the words of our Saviour that they were nearest him who believed in him?

A. St. Matt. xii. 49, 50.

" See Lucifer like lightning fall,
   Dash'd from his throne of pride ;
While answering Thy victorious call,
   The saints his spoils divide,
This world of thine, by him usurp'd too long,
Now opening all her stores to heal thy servants' wrong.

There's not a strain to memory dear,
   Nor flower in classic grove,
There's not a sweet note warbled here
   But minds us of Thy love.
O Lord, our Lord, and Spoiler of our foes,
There is no light but Thine ; with Thee all beauty glows."
Keble.

THE FOURTH SUNDAY IN LENT.

The Collect.

GRANT, we beseech thee, Almighty God, that we, who for our evil deeds do worthily deserve to be punished, by the comfort of thy grace may mercifully be relieved; through our Lord and Saviour Jesus Christ. Amen.

The Epistle. Gal. iv. 21.—*The Gospel.* St. John vi. 1.

1. Q. What is this Sunday called?

THE FOURTH SUNDAY IN LENT.

A. The Sunday of refreshment.
2. Q. Why has this name been given to it?
A. Because as Christ satisfied the hungry by the miraculous feeding, so he will feed the soul with the bread of life.
3. Q. Where is this miraculous feeding recorded?
A. St. John vi. 10, 11.
4. Q. Where is the spiritual food spoken of?
A. St. John vi. 54, 55.
1. Q. What is the design of this Sunday?
A. To teach us to hope in Jesus.
2. Q. How is this encouragement exhibited?
A. By showing us our freedom as the sons of God.
3. Q. How may we become the sons of God?
A. St. John i. 12.
4. Q. As the sons of God, how are we assured of our freedom?
A. Gal. iv. 7.
1. Q. To what do we now look forward?
A. To Christ as our Passover.
2. Q. How is Christ our Passover?
A. He was slain as the paschal lamb, to free us from our sins.
3. Q. Where is Christ said to be sacrificed as our Passover?
A. 1 Cor. v. 7.
4. Q. How are we to celebrate this event?
A. 1 Cor. v. 8.
1. Q. What therefore does the miracle in the gospel illustrate?

A. The Holy Eucharist, or Communion.
Q. What is the object of the Holy Eucharist?
A. To strengthen and refresh our souls.
Q. Where is the command given to celebrate the Holy Eucharist?
A. St. Luke xxii. 19.
Q. Is obedience to this command essential to the Christian life?
A. St. John vi. 53.
Q. What does the Holy Eucharist commemorate?
A. It shows forth the death of Christ.
Q. Why did Christ use bread and wine in this sacrament?
A. To represent his broken body and his blood shed for man.
Q. Where is this asserted in Scripture?
A. St. Mark xiv. 22, 24.
Q. Could there have been remission of sins without this sacrifice of Christ?
A. Heb. ix. 22.
Q. What is given to the worthy recipient of the Holy Eucharist?
A. Grace to keep Christ's commandments.
Q. What is meant by the unworthy reception of the sacrament?
A. Partaking of the Lord's Supper improperly, irreverently, without discerning the Lord's body.
Q. What does St. Paul say of those who receive this sacrament unworthily?
A. 1 Cor. xi. 27.

4. Q. What preparation does he urge upon Christians who are about to receive it?
A. 1 Cor. xi. 28.
1. Q. What do we confess in the collect for this day?
A. That we need God's grace.
2. Q. From what does the grace of God free us?
A. From that punishment which for our evil deeds we do worthily deserve.
3. Q. Is the grace of God sufficient to keep us from all evils and temptations?
A. 2 Cor. xii. 9.
4. Q. To whom is the grace of God promised?
A. St. James iv. 6.
1. Q. In whose name do we pray for this grace?
A. In the name of Jesus Christ our blessed Redeemer.
2. Q. Why do we pray in the name of Jesus Christ?
A. Because through the death and sufferings of Jesus Christ our pardon was procured.
3. Q. Why is calling on the name of Christ an assurance of its being given?
A. St. John i. 17.
4. Q. How extensive is the promise to those who ask in the name of Christ?
A. St. John xiv. 13.

"O help us, Lord, each hour of need
  Thy heavenly succour give;
Help us in thought, and word, and deed,
  Each hour on earth we live.

> O help us, Saviour, from on high,
>   We know no help but Thee;
> O help us so to live and die,
>   As Thine in heaven to be."
>
> *Milman.*

✗ THE FIFTH SUNDAY IN LENT.

The Collect.

WE beseech thee, Almighty God, mercifully to look upon thy people; that by thy great goodness they may be governed and preserved evermore, both in body and soul; through Jesus Christ our Lord. *Amen.*

The Epistle. Heb. ix. 11.—*The Gospel.* St. John viii. 46.

1. Q. What is this Sunday called?
   A. Passion Sunday.
2. Q. Why is this name given to the fifth Sunday in Lent?
   A. Because the story of our Lord's sufferings and death begins in the services of this day.
3. Q. Where in the Old Testament was the passion and death of Christ predicted?
   A. Isai. liii. 8.
4. Q. Where in the New Testament is this quotation referred to our blessed Redeemer?
   A. Acts viii. 32–35.
1. Q. What did Christ do for us which we celebrate at this time?
   A. He suffered, was crucified and buried.
2. Q. What was the object of the sufferings and death of our Saviour?

A. To save us from the punishment which we for our sins deserve.
3. Q. How do we know that this person who was to save us, was the same as Jesus of Nazareth?
A. St. Matt. i. 21.
4. Q. Is there no hope of salvation in any other than Jesus Christ?
A. 1 Cor. iii. 11.
1. Q. How were the Jews under the law purged from sin?
A. By the sacrifice of bulls and goats.
2. Q. How did these sacrifices wash away sins?
A. Because, as an act of faith, it reminded God of the sacrifice of his Son.
3. Q. Where is the system of the legal sacrifices recorded?
A. Numbers, xix. 9.
4. Q. How is this sacrifice under the law, used as an argument by St. Paul to prove the efficacy of the sacrifice of Christ?
A. Heb. ix. 14.
1. Q. What is it that really saves us from the punishment of sin?
A. The blood of our dear Lord.
2. Q. Where did Christ make this sacrifice for us?
A. On Calvary; a mount without the gates of Jerusalem; where he was crucified between two thieves.
3. Q. Where are we assured of forgiveness through the blood of Christ?

THE FIFTH SUNDAY IN LENT.

    A. 1 John i. 7.
4. Q. Where is the record of his crucifixion?
    A. St. Luke xxiii. 33.
1. Q. What is the sacrifice and death of Christ called
    A. The atonement.
2. Q. What do we mean by the atonement?
    A. The plan, by which the wrath of God was turned away from fallen man, through the voluntary offering of Christ.
3. Q. What does the Prophet Daniel declare of Christ?
    A. Dan. ix. 26.
4. Q. What honor, paid to Christ, does St. John record in his vision?
    A. Rev. v. 9.
1. Q. What will the blood of Christ do for those who believe in him?
    A. It will make them pure and good in the eyes of God.
2. Q. Will simple faith in Christ change our natures?
    A. No, we must believe and also show our faith by our works.
3. Q. What does St. James say of those who have faith without works?
    A. St. James ii. 14.
4. Q. What instance does he draw of believing which did not effect salvation?
    A. St. James ii. 19.
1. Q. What do we pray for in the Collect?
    A. That we may accept his mercy.

THE FIFTH SUNDAY IN LENT.

2. Q. How will his looking mercifully upon us accomplish this benefit?
A. By directing us by his Holy Spirit, so that our thoughts, words and actions may be conformable to his blessed will.
3. Q. If we believe in Christ will this directing grace be given to us?
A. St. John iii. 36.
4. Q. What further promise does Christ give to those who love him and keep his commandments?
A. St. John xiv. 21.
1. Q. Who are God's people referred to in the Collect?
A. All who have been baptized in his name.
2. Q. Are little children God's people?
A. Yes, because all who are received into his Church by baptism become his children, and promise to be faithful to his fatherly commands.
3. Q. How do we know that all such are the sons of God?
A. Rom. viii. 14.
4. Q. Is baptism one of the positive and essential commands of Christ?
A. St. John iii. 5.

"O sacred head, now wounded!
  With grief and shame weighed down
O sacred brow, surrounded
  With thorns, Thine only crown!
Once on a throne of glory,
  Adorned with light divine.
Now all despised and gory,
  I joy to call Thee mine."

THE SUNDAY NEXT BEFORE EASTER.

The Collect.

ALMIGHTY and everlasting God, who, of thy tender love towards mankind, hast sent thy Son, our Saviour Jesus Christ, to take upon him our flesh, and to suffer death upon the cross, that all mankind should follow the example of his great humility; Mercifully grant, that we may both follow the example of his patience, and also be made partakers of his resurrection; through the same Jesus Christ our Lord. *Amen.*

The Epistle. Phil. ii. 5.—*The Gospel.* St. Matt. xxvii. 1.

1. Q. By what name is this Sunday known?
   A. It is called Palm Sunday.
2. Q. From what circumstance does it derive its name?
   A. The entry of our Saviour into Jerusalem, at which time the multitude strewed palm branches before him.
3. Q. Where is this entry of Christ into Jerusalem recorded in the gospel?
   A. St. Mark xi. 8.
4. Q. Why did the disciples rejoice and praise God?
   A. St. Luke xix. 37.
1. Q. How did our blessed Lord enter Jerusalem?
   A. As the King of the whole world.
2. Q. Why did he thus enter as a king?
   A. Because, being Lord and King of the whole earth, he desired to assume the title which the prophets had foretold he should bear.

3. Q. Where and what is the prophecy of his coming into Jerusalem?
A. Zech. ix. 9.
4. Q. Where is it said that Christ should be King of the whole earth?
A. Zech. xiv. 9.
1. Q. How did the Jews receive their King?
A. With shouts of gladness.
2. Q. What were the words they used?
A. "Hosanna! Blessed is He that cometh in the name of the Lord."
3. Q. Were these shouts, which the multitude raised on the entry of Christ into Jerusalem, sincere?
A. No, for they thought that they were hailing a king who would improve their worldly condition as a nation.
4. Q. What subsequent scene proves that the Jews were insincere in their acclamations on Palm Sunday.
A. St. John xix. 5, 6.
1. Q. What did they think that Jesus had come for?
A. To be a King, like David or Solomon.
2. Q. What did the Jews expect our Saviour to do?
A. To re-establish the throne of his Father David, and rule over them with great glory and splendor.
3. Q. Give an example of such prophecies as caused the Jews to believe in a temporal Messiah?
A. Jer. xxiii. 5, 6.

THE SUNDAY NEXT BEFORE EASTER. 103

4. Q. Give an example of those prophecies concerning the coming of Christ in humility, which the Jews overlooked or misinterpreted?
A. Isaiah liii. 3.
1. Q. What was the real nature of Christ's coming as a King.
A. To be their spiritual ruler and king.
2. Q. Did the Jews understand the true nature of the Messiah?
A. No, they did not seem to know that Christ came as a spiritual and not a temporal king.
3. Q. What prophecy of Daniel made the Jews believe in the supremacy of the kingdom which Christ should establish?
A. Dan. ii. 44.
4. Q. How did our Saviour endeavor to persuade them of their error?
A. St. John xviii. 36.
1. Q. How did Jesus therefore come to proclaim his kingdom?
A. In great humility.
2. Q. Why did Christ appear in this humility and not with all the pomp of a king?
A. Because he would show how little he thought of earthly grandeur, and that his kingdom was not of this world.
3. Q. What does St. Peter say of the humility of Christ?
A. 1 St. Peter ii. 23.

4. Q. In what language did Isaiah proclaim the process of salvation through the humility of Christ?
A. Isaiah liii. 5.
1. Q. What are we therefore taught in the Collect for to-day?
A. That we should also be humble.
2. Q. How can we show our humility?
A. By being patient, and bearing meekly as our Saviour did all the trials and disappointments which may at any time befall us.
3. Q. What does our blessed Redeemer tell us to do?
A. St. Matt. xi. 29.
4. Q. How does St. Paul exhort us to patiently run our race?
A. Heb. xii. 1, 2.
1. Q. What is promised to those who follow the example of Christ's humility?
A. That they shall live with him in heaven.
2. Q. How shall we be enabled to live after the example of our Saviour?
A. By praying earnestly for the grace of the Holy Spirit in the name of Jesus Christ our Lord.
3. Q. Is there any special necessity for us to pray in the name of Jesus Christ?
A. St. John xvi. 23, 24.
4. Q. What consolation does our Saviour offer to those who suffer tribulation in this world?
A. St. John xvi. 33.

"Ride on! ride on in majesty!
Hark! all the tribes Hosanna cry.
Thine humble beast pursues his road
With palms and scattered garments strewed.

Ride on! ride on in majesty!
In lowly pomp ride on to die!
O Christ, Thy triumphs now begin
O'er captive death and conquered sin."

Mrs. Stone.

GOOD FRIDAY.

The Collects.

ALMIGHTY God, we beseech thee graciously to behold this thy family, for which our Lord Jesus Christ was contented to be betrayed, and given up into the hands of wicked men, and to suffer death upon the cross, who now liveth and reigneth with thee and the Holy Ghost, ever one God, world without end. *Amen.*

ALMIGHTY and everlasting God, by whose Spirit the whole body of the Church is governed and sanctified; Receive our supplications and prayers, which we offer before thee for all estates of men in thy holy Church, that every member of the same, in his vocation and ministry, may truly and godly serve thee; through our Lord and Saviour Jesus Christ. *Amen.*

O MERCIFUL God, who hast made all men, and hatest nothing that thou hast made, nor desirest the death of a sinner, but rather that he should be converted and live; Have mercy upon all Jews, Turks, Infidels, and Heretics; and take from them all ignorance, hardness of heart, and contempt of thy Word; and so fetch them home, blessed Lord, to thy flock, that they may be saved among the remnant of the true Israelites, and be made one fold under one shepherd; Jesus Christ our Lord, who liveth and reigneth with thee and the Holy Spirit, one God, world without end. Amen.

The Epistle. Heb. x. 1.—*The Gospel.* St. John xix. 1.

1. Q. What great event does the Church celebrate to-day?
   A. The crucifixion of Christ.
2. Q. Why is it called Good Friday?
   A. Because of the great good that we derive from the crucifixion of Christ on this day.
3. Q. Where is Christ spoken of in prophecy, as the Lamb who should be slain for us?
   A. Isai. liii. 7.
4. Q. How do we know that this sacrifice of Christ was voluntary on his part?
   A. St. John xix. 11.
1. Q. What kind of punishment was the death on the cross?
   A. A Roman punishment of nailing the person on the cross.
2. Q. What kind of criminals were usually put to death in this way?
   A. Slaves and the most depraved criminals.
3. Q. What did the soldiers who crucified him, do with the garments of Jesus?
   A. St. Matt. xxvii. 35.
4. Q. What had been said by the Psalmist concerning the disposal of his garments?
   A. Ps. xxii. 18.

1. Q. What was the character of those who were crucified with Jesus?
   A. They were two common thieves.
2. Q. Why did they crucify him in company with such abandoned characters?
   A. In order to put as much shame upon him as possible.
3. Q. Where is it stated that Christ was crucified with two malefactors?
   A. St. Luke xxiii. 33.
4. Q. What did one of the malefactors say to Jesus?
   A. St. Luke xxiii. 39.
1. Q. What flowed from the side of our Lord when the soldier pierced it?
   A. Water and blood.
2. Q. What two sacraments of the Gospel are these supposed to symbolize?
   A. The water was symbolical of Baptism, and the blood of the Holy communion.
3. Q. Recite passages in the Gospel which show the necessity of these two sacraments?
   A. St. John iii. 5; vi. 53.
4. Q. From what commandment of Christ do we believe that these sacraments must be administered by persons lawfully ordained for that purpose?
   A. St. Matt. xxviii. 19.
1. Q. Why was it necessary that Christ should die?
   A. That we might be saved from death.
2. Q. What had it been said that Christ should do?

GOOD FRIDAY.

    A. That he should "bear our sins in his own body on the tree."
3. Q. Where is it said that we are saved by the sacrifice of Christ?
    A. Heb. x. 10.
4. Q. How do we know that this sacrifice of Christ once offered is not to be repeated?
    A. Heb. x. 14.
1. Q. What should we learn from the death and sacrifice of Christ?
    A. How great our sins are that should need such a sacrifice.
2. Q. Could we not have been pardoned of our sins without the sufferings and death of our Saviour?
    A. No; for man lost all other hope of salvation through his disobedience.
3. Q. What does the Psalmist say of the sinfulness of men?
    A. Ps. xiv. 3.
4. Q. How do we know that salvation comes alone through Christ?
    A. Acts iv. 12.
1. Q. How should this blessed sacrifice of Christ affect us?
    A. It should make us love him.
2. Q. How did Christ set us an example of love even at the time of his death?
    A. By forgiving his persecutors, and praying his Father that he would pardon them.

GOOD FRIDAY.

3. Q. What was this prayer of Christ for his persecutors?
   A. St. Luke xxiii. 34.
4. Q. What words of comfort did Christ speak to the penitent thief?
   A. St. Luke xxiii. 43.
1. Q. How can we best show forth our love for Christ?
   A. By obeying his commandments?
2. Q. Is it possible for us really to love Christ and yet disobey his commands?
   A. No; love to Christ involves the idea of obedience—love therefore is not merely feeling but it includes the doing.
3. Q. What does our blessed Saviour say of all those who love him?
   A. St. John xiv. 23.
4. Q. What does the love of Christ prompt us in reference to our feeling for others?
   A. 1 John iv. 21.

" Lord of my heart, by thy last cry,
  Let not thy blood on earth be spent—
Lo, at thy feet I fainting lie,
  Mine eyes upon thy wounds are bent,
Upon thy streaming wounds my weary eyes
Wait like parched earth on April skies.

Wash me, and dry these bitter tears,
  O let my heart no further roam,
'Tis thine by vows, and hopes and fears,
  Long since; O call thy wanderer home;
To that dear home, safe in Thy wounded side,
Where only broken hearts their sin and shame may hide."
Keble.

EASTER EVEN.

The Collect.

GRANT, O Lord, that as we are baptized into the death of thy blessed Son our Saviour Jesus Christ, so by continual mortifying our corrupt affections we may be buried with him; and that through the grave, and gate of death, we may pass to our joyful resurrection; for his merits, who died, and was buried, and rose again for us, thy Son Jesus Christ our Lord. *Amen.*

The Epistle. 1 St. Pet. iii. 17.—*The Gospel.* St. Matt. xxvii. 57.

1. Q. What is the last day of Lent called?
   A. Easter Even, or the Vigil of Easter.
2. Q. Why is it called a vigil?
   A. Because the early Christians abstained from sleep on the evening before a great festival, for the purpose of holy meditation.
3. Q. Whom are we to consider in these meditations?
   A. Heb. iii. 1.
4. Q. What advantage does St. Paul point out to St. Timothy to be derived from these holy meditations?
   A. 1 Tim. iv. 15.
1. Q. What do we commemorate on this day?
   A. The time that our Saviour spent in the grave.
2. Q. Where was Christ buried?
   A. In the tomb of Joseph of Arimathæa.
3. Q. What did Joseph do when he had begged the body of Jesus?
   A. St. Matt. xxvii. 59, 60.

EASTER EVEN.

4. Q. How did the Marys show their love for their master?
A. St. Mark xvi. 1.
1. Q. What does the creed tell us that Christ did between his death and resurrection?
A. "He descended into Hell," or the place of departed spirits?
2. Q. What did our Saviour do at that time?
A. St. Peter tells us that "He went and preached to the spirits in prison."
3. Q. How does the Epistle show us that the Spirit of Christ was alive, although his body was in the grave?
A. 1 Pet. iii. 18.
4. Q. What does he say of baptism in this connection?
A. 1 Pet. iii. 21.
1. Q. If Christ was dead and buried why did the disciples watch this night?
A. Because he was to rise again?
2. Q. Did they understand what was meant by the resurrection?
A. No; but they doubtless had an idea that it referred to some great event which should come to pass on the morrow.
3. Q. How did the Chief Priests and Pharisees show that they feared the disciples would use dishonest means in establishing the truth of the resurrection of Christ?
A. St. Matt. xxvii. 64.

4. Q. What words of David did St. Peter quote as foretelling the resurrection of our Lord?
A. Acts ii. 27.
1. Q. What does the collect of the day teach us concerning ourselves?
A. That we are baptized into the death of Christ.
2. Q. What does this expression mean?
A. That by baptism we are required to die *to* all as He died *for* all sin.
3. Q. Where is the scripture proof that we are baptized into the death of Christ?
A. Rom. vi. 3.
4. Q. Where are we commanded to die unto sin?
A. Rom. vi. 11.
1. Q. What then are we instructed to do?
A. To mortify our corrupt affections.
2. Q. In what way may you overcome your evil desires?
A. By the grace of God given in baptism and constant prayer.
3. Q. What are the Colossians told to do?
A. Col. iii. 5.
4. Q. What will be the result of this mortification of the flesh?
A. Rom. viii. 13.
1. Q. On what do we place our hope, that we will " pass to our joyful resurrection?"
A. On the merits of our Lord and Saviour Jesus Christ.
2. Q. What are these merits of our Saviour?

 A. His voluntary suffering and death for us sinners, by which the justice of the Father was satisfied.

3. Q. Where are we assured that Christ died for our sins?
 A. 1 Cor. xv. 3.

4. Q. What does St. Paul tell the Romans will be our reward if we are faithful to our vows?
 A. Rom. vi. 5.

"Prisoner of Hope thou art—look up and sing
 In hope of promis'd spring.
As in the pit his father's darling lay
 Beside the desert way,
And knew not how, but knew his God would save
 Even from that living grave,
So, buried with our Lord, we'll close our eyes
To the decaying world, till Angels bid us rise."
Keble.

EASTER DAY.

The Collect.

ALMIGHTY God, who through thine only-begotten Son Jesus Christ hast overcome death, and opened unto us the gate of everlasting life; We humbly beseech thee, that, as by thy special grace preventing us thou dost put into our minds good desires, so by thy continual help we may bring the same to good effect; through Jesus Christ our Lord, who liveth and reigneth with thee and the Holy Ghost, ever one God, world without end. *Amen.*

 The Epistle. Col. iii. 1.—*The Gospel.* St. John xx. 1.

1. Q. What truth is celebrated on Easter Day?

A. The resurrection of Christ from the dead.
2. Q. From what is the word Easter derived?
A. From the old Saxon word Oster, which means "to rise."
3. Q. Who was the first to discover that Jesus had risen?
A. St. John xx. 1.
4. Q. What evidence, at the Sepulchre, did the angel give of the resurrection of Christ?
A. St. Mark xvi. 6.
1. Q. What great Jewish feast corresponded to Easter?
A. The feast of the Passover.
2. Q. What feast did Christ institute which corresponded with the eating of the paschal lamb?
A. The Holy Eucharist or the Sacrament of the Lord's Supper.
3. Q. What Prophet speaks of our Saviour as the real paschal lamb.
A. Isaiah liii. 7.
4. Q. Where does St. Paul recognize Christ as our Passover?
A. 1 Cor. v. 7.
1. Q. How did the Chief Priests try to disprove the fact that Christ rose from the dead?
A. By bribing the guards to say that while they slept, Christ's disciples stole his body.
2. Q. Did the soldiers tell this false story?
A. Yes; "and this saying is reported among the Jews till this day."

3. Q. How did Jesus prove to his disciples that it was really He who had risen?
A. St. Luke xxiv. 39.
4. Q. What did St. Thomas demand before he would believe?
A. St. John xx. 25.
1. Q. What great event took place at this time?
A. The vail of the Temple was rent from top to bottom.
2. Q. What other startling occurrence transpired?
A. Many graves were opened, and saints arose from the dead.
3. Q. Where are these facts recorded.
A. St. Matt. xxvii. 51, 52.
4. Q. How do we know that these bodies did not rise until after the resurrection of Christ?
A. 1 Cor. xv. 20.
1. Q. What was one of the first things that Christ did on meeting the Apostles after his resurrection?
A. He sent them into the world to preach in his name.
2. Q. What should this teach us?
A. The necessity and sacredness of the office of the holy ministry.
3. Q. What were the words of his commission?
A. St. Matt. xxviii. 19.
4. Q. What does St. Paul say of those who should be called to the work of the Christian Priesthood?
A. Heb. v. 4.

EASTER DAY.

1. Q. Of what truth does the resurrection of Christ assure us?
   A. That our bodies shall also rise again.
2. Q. How does St. Paul illustrate the resurrection of our bodies?
   A. By the growth of the flower from the seed, changed and beautified in form, but the same in kind.
3. Q. How does he further speak of this change in our bodies?
   A. Phil. iii. 21.
4. Q. What did our Saviour say of our resurrection?
   A. St. John v. 28, 29.
1. Q. What do we say in the Collect that Christ has done for us?
   A. That he has overcome death.
2. Q. How did our Saviour accomplish this result?
   A. By receiving death, the penalty of sin himself, and thus destroying the power of death.
3. Q. What does St. Paul say is the sting of death?
   A. 1 Cor. xv. 56.
4. Q. What comfortable assurance does the Apostle give to those who have gained the victory through Jesus Christ?
   A. 1 Cor. xv. 58.
1. Q. How was Christ the victor over death and the grave?
   A. By rising by his own power after he had submitted voluntarily to death.

2. Q. How has this opened to us the gate of everlasting life?
A. Because God has accepted the sacrifice of Christ, which was made that we might live.

3. Q. If we are risen with Christ what are we expected to do?
A. Col. iii. 1.

4. Q. Can we do this of our own strength?
A. Rom. viii. 26.

> "Oh! day of days! shall hearts set free
> No 'minstrel rapture' find for Thee?
> Thou art the Sun of other days,
> They shine by giving back thy rays:
>
> Enthroned in thy sovereign sphere
> Thou shedd'st thy light on all the year:
> Sundays by Thee more glorious break,
> An Easter Day in every week:
>
> And work-days, following in their train,
> The fulness of thy blessing gain,
> Till all, both resting and employ,
> Be one Lord's day of holy joy."
>
> *Keble.*

THE FIRST SUNDAY AFTER EASTER.

The Collect.

ALMIGHTY Father, who hast given thine only Son to die for our sins, and to rise again for our justification; Grant us so to put away the leaven of malice and wickedness, that we may always serve thee in pureness of living and truth; through the merits of the same thy Son Jesus Christ our Lord. *Amen.*

THE FIRST SUNDAY AFTER EASTER.

The Epistle. 1 St. John v. 4.—*The Gospel.* St. John xx. 19.

1. Q. What is this Sunday sometimes called?
   A. Low Sunday, or the Sunday of Albs.
2. Q. Why is it called by these names?
   A. Low Sunday because it is the first of the lower Easters, which we keep every week. Sunday of Albs, from the ancient custom of the baptized appearing at Church in the Albs or white garments given to them at their baptism.
3. Q. In what spiritual sense does Isaiah speak of the wearing of robes?
   A. Isaiah lxi. 10.
4. Q. What did the white robes in St. John's vision signify?
   A. Rev. vii. 14.
1. Q. What is said in the Epistle of those who are born of God?
   A. That they have overcome the world?
2. Q. What do you mean by overcoming the world?
   A. Conquering our worldly desires and affections.
3. Q. Where do we find this truth in Scripture?
   A. Rom. viii. 37.
4. Q. What will be given to those who overcome the world?
   A. Rev. ii. 7.
1. Q. How is the world to be overcome?
   A. Through faith in our Lord Jesus Christ.
2. Q. Is faith simply belief in Christ?
   A. No; it is belief joined with a purpose of obeying Him.

3. Q. How does St. Paul describe faith?
A. Heb. xi. 1.
4. Q. What did our Saviour say of the power of faith?
A. St. Luke xvii. 6.
1. Q. What did the death and resurrection of Christ gain for us?
A. Our justification before God?
2. Q. What do you mean by being justified before God?
A. That we are reconciled to God as though we or our fathers had never offended him by sin.
3. Q. What does the Prophet Isaiah say concerning our justification through Christ?
A. Isaiah xlv. 25.
4. Q. What is said to the Corinthians of the fulness of our justification by Christ?
A. 1 Cor. vi. 11.
1. Q. Where were you first justified?
A. In the waters of baptism by which our original sin was washed away.
2. Q. Does baptism justify the sinner in the highest sense?
A. No; we must repent and believe and continue faithful to the end of our lives, or else we shall not be partakers of this justification.
3. Q. How do we know that faith and baptism are both required?
A. St. John iii. 5.
4. Q. What does our Saviour promise to those who are faithful to the end?

A. St. Matt. xxiv. 13.
1. Q. What do we acknowledge in the Collect that we must do?
A. We must put away the leaven of malice and wickedness.
2. Q. What is leaven?
A. Literally it is a piece of sour dough.
3. Q. Does St. Paul speak of this leaven as being opposite to sincerity and truth?
A. 1 Cor. v. 8.
4. Q. In what connection does our Saviour refer to leaven?
A. St. Matt. xiii. 33; xvi. 6.
1. Q. What does the gospel tell us that Christ said to his disciples?
A. "As my Father hath sent me even so send I you."
2. Q. Is Christ ever called in the Bible an Apostle, or "one sent?"
A. Yes; St. Paul calls him "the Apostle and High Priest" of our profession.
3. Q. For what purpose did Christ send forth his ministers?
A. St. Mark xvi. 15.
4. Q. Did the Apostles have power to send others as they were sent?
A. 2 Tim. ii. 2.
1 Q. What special power did Christ here give to his Priests?
A. The declaration of the forgiveness of sins.

2. Q. Can the minister forgive sins of himself?
A. No; he does it by "the power and commandment" which he received from Christ.
3. Q. Repeat the words where our Saviour gave this "power and commandment."
A. St. John xx. 23.
4. Q. How do we know that the Church teaches that her Priests have this power?
A. Because in "the ordering of Priests" when the Bishop lays his hands on the head of the candidate, he solemnly and in the name of Christ, repeats the words of our Saviour.

"By his word and by his hour
When the promise came with power—
By his Holy Spirit's token,
By his saintly chain unbroken,
Lengthening, while his world lasts on,
From his cross unto his throne—
Guardians of his Virgin spouse!
Know that His might is yours, whose breathing sealed your vows."

THE SECOND SUNDAY AFTER EASTER.

The Collect.

ALMIGHTY God, who hast given thine only Son to be unto us both a sacrifice for sin, and also an ensample of godly life; Give us grace that we may always most thankfully receive that his inestimable benefit, and also daily endeavour ourselves to follow the blessed steps of his most holy life; through the same Jesus Christ our Lord. *Amen.*

The Epistle. 1 St. Pet. ii. 19.—*The Gospel.* St. John x. 11.

1. Q. How was Christ a sacrifice for sin?
   A. By dying on the cross for sin.
2. Q. What made the sacrifice of Christ necessary to our salvation?
   A. The disobedience of man, by which death came into the world.
3. Q. How do we know that as by Adam we inherited death, so in Christ we shall receive life?
   A. 1 Cor. xv. 21, 22.
4. Q. Could there have been no remission of sin without the death of Christ?
   A. Heb. ix. 22.

1. Q. What beside a sacrifice for sin does the Collect tell us our Saviour was?
   A. An example of godly life.
2. Q. In what way was He an example?
   A. By exhibiting in his life every virtue and grace.
3. Q. What does St. Paul say of the sinless character of Jesus?
   A. Heb. iv. 15.
4. Q. Did any other perfect human being ever live besides Christ?
   A. Ps. xiv. 3.

1. Q. What must we do to receive the benefit of the sacrifice of Christ?
   A. We must endeavour to follow his example.
2. Q. How can we follow so perfect a pattern?
   A. By the assistance of the Holy Ghost, though imperfectly at best.

THE SECOND SUNDAY AFTER EASTER. 123

3. Q. Are we promised the assistance of the Holy Spirit?
A. St. John xvi. 13.
4. Q. How are we taught to build ourselves up in our most holy faith?
A. St. Jude 20, 21.
1. Q. What does our Saviour call himself in the gospel?
A. The good Shepherd.
2. Q. In what way, according to his own figure, did he show that he was a good Shepherd?
A. By giving up his life for his sheep.
3. Q. Had any of the Prophets spoken of the Messiah as a Shepherd?
A. Isaiah xl. 11.
4. Q. Where is Christ recognized as *the* Shepherd above all others?
A. Heb. xiii. 20.
1. Q. What are we called in the "Jubilate?"
A. "The sheep of his pasture."
2. Q. In what part of the Church service do we compare ourselves to sheep?
A. In the confession, where we acknowledge that "we have strayed from his ways like lost sheep."
3. Q. What are the Bishops and Pastors of Christ's flock instructed to do?
A. 1 St. Pet. v. 2.
4. Q. Are we to follow Christ as sheep follow their Shepherd?

A. St. John xii. 26.
1. Q. Who were peculiarly Christ's sheep at the time that he said these words?
A. The Jews.
2. Q. Whom did he mean by the "other sheep?"
A. The Gentiles, or all born out of the Jewish nation.
3. Q. How do we know that He referred to the Gentiles?
A. Eph. iii. 5, 6.
4. Q. Where is it intimated in the Old Testament that Gentiles should be included in his fold?
A. Isaiah xlix. 6.
1. Q. What did Christ mean the sheepfold to represent?
A. His visible Church on earth.
2. Q. What do we call it in the creed?
A. "The one Catholic and Apostolic Church."
3. Q. By what sacrament are persons admitted into his Church?
A. By the holy Sacrament of Baptism, by which "they are regenerate and grafted into the body of Christ's Church."
4. Q. What did Christ pray might be accomplished among all persons calling themselves Christians?
A. St. John xvii. 21.
1. Q. What other Sacrament did our Saviour institute just before his death?
A. The Sacrament of the Lord's Supper.

2. Q. How often did the early Christians celebrate the Holy Eucharist?
A. Very frequently daily and always weekly.
3. Q. What did St. Paul say that we should do this for?
A. 1 Cor. xi. 26.
4. Q. Where does Jesus affirm that this Sacrament is necessary to everlasting life?
A. St. John vi. 53.

"The Lord is our Shepherd, our Guardian, and Guide;
Whatever we want he will kindly provide,
To sheep of his pasture his mercies abound,
His care and protection his flock will surround."
Lit. and Hymns.

THE THIRD SUNDAY AFTER EASTER.

The Collect.

ALMIGHTY God, who showest to them that are in error the light of thy truth, to the intent that they may return into the way of righteousness; grant unto all those who are admitted into the fellowship of CHRIST's religion, that they may avoid those things that are contrary to their profession, and follow all such things as are agreeable to the same, through our Lord JESUS CHRIST. *Amen.*

The Epistle. 1. St. Peter ii. 11.—*The Gospel.* St. John xvi. 16.

1. Q. What do we acknowledge in the collect for this day?
A. That God will show us His truth.
2. Q. What is "the light of His truth"?
A. Those doctrines which he gave us for our salvation.
3. Q. What does St. John say was the true light?

A. St. John i. 9.
4. Q. Did Christ promise that we should be able to know what his truth was?
A. St. John viii. 32.
1. Q. How can we learn the truth of Christ?
A. By reading and meditating on His word, the Holy Bible.
2. Q. How do we know what are the truths of the Bible?
A. By listening to the voice of the Church, which is called in Scripture "the pillar and ground of the truth."
3. Q. How do we know that the Bible contains all the truths necessary to our salvation?
A. 2 Tim. iii. 16.
4. Q. From what do we infer, that we should be guided in our Bible reading by the voice of the Church?
A. 2 St. Pet. i. 20.
1. Q. Who are those "that are in error"?
A. All who are not truly Christians.
2. Q. May those who believe all the Christian doctrines, be nevertheless in error?
A. Yes, unless they not only believe but live according to those doctrines.
3. Q. How much disobedience constitutes absolute guilt?
A. St. James ii. 10.
4. Q. What does St. James say is necessary besides faith?

A. St. James ii. 26.
1. Q. What therefore are we called upon to do in the Epistle?
A. To "abstain from fleshly lusts."
2. Q. What do you mean by fleshly lusts?
A. All those evil desires which war against the soul.
3. Q. What does St. Paul tell the Galatians about the contention of the flesh and the spirit?
A. Gal. v. 17.
4. Q. What therefore does he tell St. Timothy to do?
A. 1 St. Tim. vi. 11.
1. Q. What does Jesus tell his disciples in the gospel?
A. That in a little while they should not see him.
2. Q. Did they understand what he meant?
A. No, for they said, "we cannot tell what he saith."
3. Q. When did Jesus in reality go to the Father?
A. St. Mark xvi. 19.
4. Q. For what purpose will our Saviour return again?
A. St. John xiv. 3.
1. Q. What did Christ say should follow his leaving them?
A. They should weep and lament.
2. Q. Why should they be thus sorrowful?
A. Because they did not fully understand how and why he should be taken from them.
3. Q. How at his death did the disciples show their sorrow?
A. St. Luke xxiii. 27.
4. Q. When was their sorrow turned into joy?

A. St. John xx. 20.
1. Q. What should afterwards be a cause of joy?
  A. That they should see him again.
2. Q. How can we participate in that joy of the disciples?
  A. By beholding Christ with the eye of faith.
3. Q. When did the blessed Redeemer promise to reveal himself to us?
  A. Rev. iii. 20.
4. Q. What presence of Christ shall be our greatest joy?
  A. Phil. i. 23.
1. Q. How long was this joy to remain?
  A. "Your joy no man taketh from you."
2. Q. When shall we realize this joy to the fullest?
  A. In heaven, where we shall ever remain in his presence.
3. Q. May we experience this joy even without seeing Christ?
  A. 1 St. Pet. i. 8.
4. Q. What evidence have we that the Apostles fully understood the truth of the resurrection?
  A. Acts iv. 10; v. 31.

" Lord, come to us, unloose our bands,
  And bid our terrors cease;
Lift over us Thy blessed hands:
  Speak, holy Jesus, Peace.

And hear Thy saints, who to Thee pray
  To bring them to their home;
Hear, when the Bride and Spirit say,
  'Come, blessed Jesus, come!'"

Huntington.

THE FOURTH SUNDAY AFTER EASTER.

The Collect.

O ALMIGHTY God, who alone canst order the unruly wills and affections of sinful men; Grant unto thy people, that they may love the thing which thou commandest, and desire that which thou dost promise; that so, among the sundry and manifold changes of the world, our hearts may surely there be fixed, where true joys are to be found; through Jesus Christ our Lord. *Amen.*

The Epistle. St. James i. 17.—*The Gospel.* St. John xvi. 5.

1. Q. What are we taught this day?
   A. That we cannot do right of ourselves.
2. Q. Who alone can give us the strength to do right?
   A. God, through the influence of his Holy Spirit.
3. Q. What does the Epistle tell us of all the good gifts which we receive?
   A. St. Jas. i. 17.
4. Q. What did St. Paul find resisting his inclinations to do good?
   A. Rom. vii. 21.
1. Q. What is it that prevents us from doing good?
   A. Our "unruly wills and affections."
2. Q. What are these "unruly wills and affections"?
   A. The evil thoughts and desires which are born of Satan.
3. Q. What does Solomon say of the thoughts of the wicked?
   A. Prov. xv. 26.

4. Q. What does David pray God to do?
A. Ps. cxxxix. 23, 24.
1. Q. What do we pray for in the Collect?
A. That we may love the things which God has commanded.
2. Q. How can our love for the commandments of God be shown?
A. By cheerfully obeying all his laws.
3. Q. What great laws were given to the Jewish nation?
A. The decalogue, or ten commandments, which were received by Moses from God on Mount Sinai.
4. Q. On what two commandments did our Saviour say "hung all the law and the Prophets"?
A. St. Matt. xxii. 37–40.
1. Q. Why do we pray that we may keep God's commands?
A. That we may receive joy from God.
2. Q. Where are these true joys to be found?
A. In holy living in this world, and in the presence of the Triune God in heaven.
3. Q. Where are we told to set our affections?
A. Col. iii. 2.
4. Q. What is said of the joy in the presence of God?
A. Ps. xvi. 11.
1. Q. In order to learn this obedience to God's commandments what ought we be ready to do?
A. We should be *willing* to learn.
2. Q. How does the Epistle tell us we should act?

THE FOURTH SUNDAY AFTER EASTER.

A. "Be swift to hear, slow to speak, slow to wrath."
3. Q. What does St. James exhort us to do?
A. St. Jas. i. 21.
4. Q. What does St. Paul say is necessary to the success of our Christian race?
A. Heb. xii. 1.
1. Q. When Christ should ascend to heaven who was to remind them of their duty?
A. The Holy Ghost, the Comforter.
2. Q. What would the Comforter do?
A. He would "guide them into all truth."
3. Q. Where are we assured that the Holy Ghost was sent to the disciples?
A. Acts xiii. 52.
4. Q. How did Christ show that the Holy Spirit would guide his Church in his stead?
A. St. Matt. xxviii. 20.
1. Q. What else would the Comforter do?
A. He would "reprove the world of sin."
2. Q. In what way had the world especially sinned?
A. By denying the Lord that bought them.
3. Q. How universal was the wickedness of the world?
A. 1 St. John v. 19.
4. Q. What is the result of the denial of Christ?
A. St. John iii. 18.
1. Q. What part did the Holy Spirit take in writing the Bible?
A. He put the truth into the minds of the writers.
2. Q. When Christ sent forth his disciples what did he tell them of the truth which they should speak?

A. "It is not ye that speak, but the spirit of your father which speaketh in you."
3. Q. What did St. Paul acknowledge to the Corinthians?
A. 1 Cor. ii. 13.
4. Q. What did St. Peter say of the writing of the Old Testament?
A. 2 St. Pet. i. 21.

"Soft as the plumes of Jesus' Dove
They nurse the soul to heavenly love;
The struggling spark of good within,
Just smothered in the strife of sin,
They quicken to a timely glow,
The pure flame spreading high and low.
Said I, that prayer and hope were o'er?
Nay, blessed Spirit! but by Thee
The Church's prayer finds wings to soar,
The Church's hope finds eyes to see."

Keble.

THE FIFTH SUNDAY AFTER EASTER.

The Collect.

O LORD, from whom all good things do come; grant to us thy humble servants, that by thy holy inspiration we may think those things that are good, and by thy merciful guiding may perform the same, through our Lord JESUS CHRIST. *Amen.*

The Epistle. St. James i. 22.—*The Gospel.* St. John xvi. 23.

1. Q. What is this Sunday called?
A. Rogation Sunday.
2. Q. Why was it called by this name?
A. Rogation and Litany being words of the same meaning, it was used to denote the earnest

prayer which this Sunday teaches us is necessary.

3. Q. What great season does this Sunday and the next three days end?
A. The joyful season of Easter?

4. Q. To what high festival do we look forward?
A. The festival of the Ascension, when Christ was to leave the earth and go to the Father.

1. Q. In what are we instructed in the gospel?
A. Of the duty of prayer.

2. Q. What is prayer to God?
A. The earnest asking for the blessings of God.

3. Q. Where are we taught our obligations to pray?
A. Philip. iv. 6.

4. Q. How often did King David pray?
A. Ps. lv. 17.

1. Q. In whose name are we taught to pray?
A. In the name of Jesus Christ.

2. Q. In what prayers alone does the Church not pray in his name?
A. In those prayers addressed to himself or the Holy Ghost.

3. Q. In what words had the disciples been instructed to pray before this time?
A. St. Matt. vi. 9–13.

4. Q. How did holy men pray before our Saviour's time?
A. Jer. xiv. 7.

1. Q. How much will we receive if we pray in the name of Christ?

A. Every thing that we ask.
2. Q. Why then do good men sometimes pray in vain ?
A. Because they do not pray in faith.
3. Q. What did our Saviour say should be the measure of the answer to prayer ?
A. St. John xvi. 23.
4. Q. What reason does St. James give for our not receiving those things which we ask?
A. St. Jas. iv. 3.
1. Q. What is necessary to a favorable reception of our prayers?
A. That we should be humble and in earnest.
2. Q. What illustration did our Saviour give of the difference of the spirit in which prayer was offered ?
A. The pharisee, who prayed with pride in his heart, and the publican, who smote his breast crying "God be merciful to me a sinner."
3. Q. What did our Saviour say of the prayer of the publican ?
A. St. Luke xviii. 14.
4. Q. What did Christ say that God would not hear?
A. St. John ix. 31.
1. Q. What effect has prayer upon us?
A. It makes us more willing to obey God.
2. Q. What does it assist us to bear ?
A. All that God may put upon us whether of joy or sorrow.
3. Q. What does St. Paul confess of the sufficiency of grace ?

THE FIFTH SUNDAY AFTER EASTER.

A. 2 Cor. xii. 9.

4. Q. What words of our Saviour declare the necessity of private as well as public prayer?
A. St. Matt. vi. 6.

1. Q. What do we especially pray for in the Collect to-day?
A. That "we may think those things that are good."

2. Q. Where in the Church service do we pray that God may cleanse our thoughts?
A. In the prayer at the beginning of the Communion service.

3. Q. Can we sin by thought as well as by deed?
A. Prov. xxiv. 9.

4. Q. What is one of the first things that the Prophet calls upon the wicked to do?
A. Isaiah lv. 7.

1. Q. What is necessary for us, besides thinking those things that are right?
A. We must also do all that our good thoughts suggest.

2. Q. What does St. James say of those who hear but do not do?
A. That they deceive themselves if they think they have done all that they should.

3. Q. How does St. James say that faith is made perfect?
A. St. Jas. ii. 22.

4. Q. What is pure religion and undefiled before God?
A. St. Jas. i. 27.

"Lord, teach us how to pray aright,
  With reverence and with fear;
Though dust and ashes in Thy sight,
  We may, we must draw near:
We perish if we cease from prayer,
  O grant us power to pray;
And, when to meet Thee we prepare,
  Lord, meet us by the way."

Montgomery.

THE ASCENSION-DAY.

The Collect.

GRANT, we beseech thee, Almighty GOD, that like as we do believe thy only begotten Son our Lord JESUS CHRIST to have ascended into the heavens; so we may also in heart and mind thither ascend, and with him continually dwell, who liveth and reigneth with thee and the HOLY GHOST, one GOD, world without end. *Amen.*

The Epistle. Acts i. 1.—*The Gospel.* St. Mark xvi. 14.

1. Q. On what day in the week did our Saviour ascend into heaven?
   A. On Thursday.
2. Q. How many days was the ascension after Easter?
   A. Forty days.
3. Q. What office does Christ exercise for us in heaven?
   A. Heb. vii. 25.
4. Q. What prophecy looks forward to the ascension of Christ?
   A. Ps. lxviii. 18.
1. Q. From what place did Jesus ascend?
   A. From the Mount of Olives.
2. Q. Did his body ascend, or only his Spirit?

THE ASCENSION-DAY.

  A. The same body ascended, which he took at first and was crucified for us on Calvary.
3. Q. How do we prove this fact?
  A. St. Luke xxiv. 51.
4. Q. What evidence did the two angels give of his ascension?
  A. Acts i. 11.
1. Q. Did any man ascend to the heavens before Christ?
  A. Not in the same sense.
2. Q. What were the names of those who were translated or carried up bodily without death?
  A. Enoch, Elijah, and some think Moses also.
3. Q. What was the peculiarity of the ascension of Christ?
  A. Eph. iv. 8.
4. Q. What act was our Saviour performing at the time of His ascension?
  A. St. Luke xxiv. 50.
1. Q. What do we pray for in the Collect?
  A. That we may ascend with Christ, in our hearts.
2. Q. What does this mean?
  A. That our hearts may be fit to ascend with Him.
3. Q. What will assist us in our preparation to meet Him in the heavens?
  A. Col. iii. 2, 4.
4. Q. How do we know that if we are faithful, we shall ascend and be with Christ?
  A. 1 Thes. iv. 17.

1. Q. How can we ascend to heaven in mind and heart?
A. By thinking of heavenly things and fitting ourselves for heaven.
2. Q. How can we do this, while we are yet on earth?
A. By separating ourselves from worldly things and living as if we were really in the presence of Christ.
3. Q. Where is the conversation of the faithful said to be?
A. Phil. iii. 20.
4. Q. Does not St. Paul seem to intimate that it is possible for us by God's grace to become almost sinless?
A. Rom. vi. 2.
1. Q. Will our Lord ever return to earth again?
A. Yes; to judge the world.
2. Q. Do we know the exact time when He will make His appearance?
A. No, for He nowhere informs us of the time of his coming again.
3. Q. What did Christ say on this subject?
A. St. Matt. xxiv. 36.
4. Q. What does He therefore tell us is our duty?
A. St. Matt. xxiv. 44.
1. Q. Where is our Saviour at this time?
A. Sitting at the right hand of God.
2. Q. What does he do for us in heaven?
A. He ever liveth to make intercession for us.

THE ASCENSION-DAY.

3. Q. Where are we told of the work of Christ for us at the throne of the Father?
A. Rom. viii. 34.

4. Q. How does the intercession of Christ make the salvation of the faithful infallibly certain?
A. Heb. vii. 25.

1. Q. When Christ comes again how will He appear?
A. In the clouds with great glory.

2. Q. What is the day of His coming called?
A. The judgment; when He will decide between the righteous and the wicked.

3. Q. Where in the New Testament, is the Second Coming of Christ described?
A. St. Matt. xxiv. 30.

4. Q. What did St. John in his vision, see of the glory of that day?
A. Rev. i. 7.

" Crown the Saviour, angels crown Him;
Rich the trophies, Jesus brings;
On the Seat of power enthrone Him,
While the heavenly concert rings:
Crown Him;
Crown the Saviour King of Kings."

Kelley.

" O Thou, who thus exalted art,
On whom our souls rely,
Grant to us now, in mind and heart,
To dwell with Thee on high!

And when at length, redeem'd by Thee,
The just that sleep shall rise;
With theirs our happy portion be,
A home beyond the skies."

SUNDAY AFTER ASCENSION-DAY.
The Collect.

O GOD, the King of glory, who hast exalted thine only Son Jesus Christ with great triumph unto thy kingdom in heaven; We beseech thee, leave us not comfortless; but send to us thine Holy Ghost to comfort us, and exalt us unto the same place whither our Saviour Christ is gone before, who liveth and reigneth with thee and the Holy Ghost, one God, world without end. *Amen.*

The Epistle. 1 St. Pet. iv. 7.—*The Gospel.* St. John xv. 26. *and part of chap.* xvi.

1. Q. What is this Sunday called?
   A. Expectation Sunday.
2. Q. Why is it called by this name?
   A. Because the Apostles were expecting the fulfillment of the promise "If I go away I will send the Comforter to you."
3. Q. Where had the promise of the Comforter been given to them?
   A. St. John xvi. 7.
4. Q. Where is the coming of the Holy Ghost prophesied in the Old Testament?
   A. Joel ii. 28, 29.
1. Q. With what feelings did the disciples behold their Lord ascend?
   A. With feelings of great joy.
2. Q. Why did they not manifest sorrow as at the time of his death?
   A. Because Christ had instructed them that He

would always be present with them in the person of the Holy Ghost.

3. Q. What promise did they now perceive referred to the Holy Spirit?
A. St. Matt. xxviii. 20.

4. Q. Where is the Holy Ghost spoken of as being coeternal with the Father and the Son?
A. Heb. ix. 14.

1. Q. What do you mean by praying that you may not be left comfortless?
A. That the Comforter may come to us as he did to the Apostles.

2. Q. Who do you mean by the Comforter?
A. The Holy Ghost, the third person in the adorable Trinity.

3. Q. You say the third person; is the Holy Ghost, equal with the Father and Son?
A. 1 St. John v. 7.

4. Q. What benediction shows the equality of the three persons in the Godhead?
A. 2 Cor. xiii. 14.

1. Q. What virtue is especially recommended at this time?
A. Charity or love for each other.

2. Q. Why is this brought to our notice at this time?
A. Because the Holy Spirit which is love, could not operate upon an unloving heart.

3. Q. What is said to be the fruit of the Spirit?
A. Gal. v. 22, 23.

4. Q. Is charity among ourselves obligatory as well as our love to God?
A. 1 John iv. 21.
1. Q. Of what duty are we here reminded?
A. To work for Christ as we are able.
2. Q. What is required of each one of us?
A. To minister according to the gifts which we have received.
3. Q. What kind of gifts has God given to men in his Church?
A. 1 Cor. xii. 28.
4. Q. How does the Epistle say that we should work?
A. 1 St. Pet. iv. 11.
1. Q. When the Holy Ghost should come, what would He do?
A. He would testify of Christ.
2. Q. How would He testify of Christ?
A. By coming in a miraculous manner as Christ had said.
3. Q. Was this promise fulfilled?
A. Acts ii. 3, 4.
4. Q. How is this testimony of the Holy Ghost conveyed to us?
A. 2 Cor. i. 12.
1. Q. Who else were to bear witness to the truth of Christ?
A. His Apostles and their successors.
2. Q. How were they to bear witness of him?
A. By teaching the truth which they had received from him.

3. Q. In what words did our Lord give them the authority to preach in his name?
A. St. Mark xvi. 15.
4. Q. Did the Apostles go forth under this commission?
A. St. Mark xvi. 20.
1. Q. How did they testify of Jesus besides teaching his truth?
A. By suffering and dying for the truth.
2. Q. Who was the first Christian martyr?
A. St. Stephen, who was a Deacon.
3. Q. Who was the first among the Apostles to suffer death for the truth's sake?
A. Acts xii. 2.
4. Q. Are we commanded to suffer martyrdom rather than to deny Christ and his truth?
A. Phil. i. 29.

"Thou art gone up on high
To mansions in the skies,
And round Thy throne unceasingly
The songs of praise arise.
But we are lingering here,
With sin and care oppressed;
Lord! send Thy promised Comforter,
And lead us to Thy rest."

WHITSUNDAY.

The Collect.

O GOD, who as at this time didst teach the hearts of thy faithful people, by sending to them the light of thy Holy Spirit; Grant us by the same Spirit to have a right judgment in all things, and evermore to rejoice in his holy comfort; through the merits of Christ Jesus our Saviour, who liveth and reigneth with thee, in the unity of the same Spirit, one God world without end. *Amen.*

For the Epistle. Acts ii. 1.—*The Gospel.* St. John xiv. 15.

1. Q. By what name is this Sunday known among Christians?
   A. By the name of Whitsunday.
2. Q. With what great feast of the Jews did Whitsunday correspond?
   A. With the feast of the Pentecost, which was celebrated fifty days after the Passover.
3. Q. How do we know that these two festivals came at the same time?
   A. Acts ii. 1.
4. Q. Where is the time set for the celebration of the feast of the Pentecost?
   A. Levit. xxiii. 15, 16.
1. Q. What event does the Christian celebrate this day?
   A. The descent of the Holy Ghost.
2. Q. What event did the Jews celebrate on the day of Pentecost?
   A. The giving of the law by Moses on Mount Sinai.
3. Q. Where had the promise of the Holy Ghost been given?
   A. Acts i. 8.
4. Q. How did the Jews keep the feast of weeks or Pentecost?
   A. Deut. xvi. 10.

1. Q. Why has this Sunday been called Whitsunday?
   A. Because on this day, those in the early Church who had been baptized appeared in white.
2. Q. What other reference has it?
   A. To the light of heaven which on this day descended upon the Church.
3. Q. Where are white garments recognized as emblems of immaculate purity?
   A. Rev. xix. 8.
4. Q. Where is white made the emblem of Spiritual cleanness?
   A. Isaiah i. 18.
1. Q. How did the Holy Ghost manifest himself on the first Whitsunday?
   A. By a bright tongue of fire, which settled upon the heads of the Apostles.
2. Q. What peculiar power was given to the Apostles at this time?
   A. To work miracles, and to preach in languages which they had never learned.
3. Q. Does this power still continue with the gift of the Holy Ghost?
   A. No; for as the Church of Christ is fully established there is no necessity of miracles to further testify of its truth.
4. Q. How does the Holy Spirit come to us now?
   A. 2 Cor. iv. 6.
1. Q. Had not the Holy Ghost been felt in the hearts of men before this time?
   A. Yes; but not with the power now given.

2. Q. Had our Saviour promised especial power at the coming of the Holy Ghost?
A. Yes; He had said that they should work miracles and speak with tongues.
3. Q. Was this gift confined to the Apostles?
A. Acts x. 45.
4. Q. How do we know that this power continued some time in the Church?
A. 1 Cor. xii. 10.
1. Q. What is the descent of the Holy Ghost called?
A. The baptism with fire.
2. Q. When St. John the Baptist, baptized with water what did he promise?
A. That Christ should baptize with the Holy Ghost and with fire.
3. Q. What does fire represent in the vision of St. John?
A. Rev. iv. 5.
4. Q. What effect did the Prophet Malachi say it would have upon the soul?
A. Mal. iii. 3.
1. Q. By what Sacrament is the gift of the Holy Ghost received?
A. By the holy Sacrament of baptism.
2. Q. How is baptism sealed or ratified?
A. By the Apostolic rite of Confirmation.
3. Q. Where do you find a proof that the Holy Ghost was given in Confirmation?
A. Acts xix. 5, 6.
4. Q. Among what fundamental doctrines does St.

Paul place Confirmation or "the laying on of hands?"

A. Heb. vi. 1, 2.

1. Q. Who can obtain the gift of the Holy Spirit now?
A. Any one who will ask for it.
2. Q. What does this asking include?
A. That we should have faith and be baptized.
3. Q. What did St. Peter tell the people to do in order to be saved on the day of Pentecost
A. Acts ii. 38.
4. Q. What is our body called which should make us careful to preserve it holy unto God?
A. 1 Cor. vi. 19.

"Holy Spirit, Lord of light,
From Thy clear celestial height,
　Thy pure beaming radiance give;
Come, thou Father of the poor,
Come with treasures which endure,
　Come, Thou Light of all that live!

Thou on those who evermore
Thee confess and Thee adore,
　In Thy sevenfold gift descend;
Give them comfort when they die,
Give them life with Thee on high,
　Give them joys which never end."

TRINITY-SUNDAY

The Collect.

ALMIGHTY and everlasting GOD, who hast given unto us thy servants grace, by the confession of a true faith, to acknowledge the glory of the eternal TRINITY, and in the power of the divine Majesty to worship the Unity; we beseech thee that thou wouldest keep us steadfast in this faith, and evermore defend us from all adversities, who livest and reignest, one God, world without end. *Amen.*

For the Epistle. Rev. iv. 1.—*The Gospel.* St. John iii. 1.

1. Q. What are we taught this day?
   A. The doctrine of the adorable Trinity.
2. Q. How do we express this doctrine?
   A. That there are three persons—The Father, The Son, and The Holy Ghost in One Godhead.
3. Q. Is the word Trinity used in the Bible?
   A. No; it is a word derived from the Latin and used by the Church to designate a doctrine which is found in Scripture.
4. Q. Can we entirely comprehend this doctrine?
   A. Job. xi. 7.
1. Q. In proving the doctrine of the Trinity from the Bible, what do we first find?
   A. That our Saviour Jesus Christ is God.
2. Q. What is said of our Lord, which is only applicable to God?
   A. He is said to be the Creator, Eternal, Omnipresent, Omniscient and Omnipotent.
3. Q. Where does one of the Apostles address Him as God?
   A. St. John xx. 28.
4. Q. In what connection does David speak of Christ as God?
   A. Ps. xlv. 6.
1. Q. By what name is Jesus Christ called by St. John?

A. He is called "The Word"—"who was God."

2. Q. What makes this title peculiarly applicable to Him?
A. As words assist us in understanding each other's thoughts, so Christ as "The Word," conveys to us God's thoughts and affections for us.

3. Q. How does St. Paul prove that we have received the thoughts of God through Christ?
A. 1 Cor. ii. 16.

4. Q. Does St. John honour The Word as God?
A. St. John i. 14.

1. Q. What is the second step in proof of the doctrine of the Trinity?
A. That the Holy Ghost is called God in the Bible.

2. Q. How is the Holy Ghost spoken of in the Scriptures?
A. As being equal with the Father and the Son in all their attributes.

3. Q. Where is the Holy Ghost directly called Jehovah or God?
A. Acts v. 3, 4.

4. Q. In what sacrament is this name joined with those of the Father and the Son?
A. St. Matt. xxviii. 19.

1. Q. How many Gods does the Bible say there are?
A. There is but one God.

2. Q. Does the doctrine of the Trinity teach that there are more Gods than one?
A. No: it says there is one God in Three Persons.

3. Q. Where do you find a proof that there is but one God?
A. Isai. xxxvii. 16
4. Q. What is the very first law as given to Moses on Mt. Sinai?
A. Ex. xx. 3.
1. Q. What have we now proved from the Bible?
A. That the Father is God, the Son is God, and the Holy Ghost is God, and yet there is but one God.
2. Q. What is the doctrine of the Trinity therefore?
A. A mystery which is beyond our comprehension.
3. Q. What intimations are given in the Old Testament of the plurality of the Godhead?
A. Read—Gen. i. 26; iii. 22. Isai. xlviii. 16.
4. Q. Do we find in our translation of the New Testament any direct proof of the Trinity?
A. 1 St. John v. 7.
1. Q. Is there any reason for denying this doctrine because we cannot understand it?
A. No; there are many mysteries which we believe but cannot understand.
2. Q. What is a mystery?
A. A truth which can only be partly understood.
3. Q. Can you give an illustration of a mystery?
A. (Let each pupil give an illustration from every-day experience.)
4. Q. In the doctrine of the resurrection, what mystery does St. Paul show the Corinthians?
A. 1 Cor. xv. 51. 52.

1. Q. Why is this doctrine essential to our faith?
   A. Because our salvation depends upon the offices of the three persons in the Trinity.
2. Q. How are we practically to apply this doctrine?
   A. "By honouring the Father who has made us; loving the Son who has redeemed us; and praying the Holy Ghost to sanctify us."
3. Q. What grace do we implore therefore at the close of our prayers?
   A. 2 Cor. xiii. 14.
4. Q. What are we exhorted to contend for?
   A. St. Jude 3.

" Holy, Holy, Holy! Lord God Almighty!
Early in the morning our songs shall rise to thee;
Holy, Holy, Holy! merciful and mighty!
God in three persons, blessed Trinity!

Holy, Holy, Holy! all the saints adore Thee,
Casting down their golden crowns around the glassy sea;
Cherubim and Seraphim falling down before Thee,
Which wert, and art, and evermore shall be!

Holy, Holy, Holy! though the darkness hide Thee,
Though the eye of sinful man Thy glory may not see,
Only Thou art Holy; there is none beside Thee,
Perfect in power, in love, in purity!"

THE FIRST SUNDAY AFTER TRINITY.

The Collect.

O GOD, the strength of all those who put their trust in thee; Mercifully accept our prayers; and because, through the weakness of our mortal nature, we can do no good thing without thee, grant us the help of thy grace, that in keeping thy commandments we may please thee, both in will and deed, through JESUS CHRIST our Lord. *Amen.*

The Epistle. 1 St. John iv. 7.—*The Gospel.* St. Luke xvi. 19.

1. Q. What have we been studying during the first part of the Christian year?
 A. The life of Christ and the doctrines of our holy religion.
2. Q. What were the chief features in the life of Christ?
 A. His incarnation, manifestation to the gentiles, circumcision, sufferings, death and resurrection.
3. Q. What else have we celebrated?
 A. The coming of the Holy Ghost, and the mystery of the Holy Trinity.
4. Q. What are we taught that we have become by this marvelous procession of events?
 A. Rom. vi. 18.
1. Q. What are we to learn during the remainder of the year?
 A. To apply these truths to our lives.
2. Q. How may we apply these truths to our lives?
 A. By praying for the Holy Spirit, to believe and do those things which Christ commanded.
3. Q. What does St. John say of those who keep Christ's commandments?
 A. 1 St. John iii. 24.

THE FIRST SUNDAY AFTER TRINITY.   153

4. Q. What does Solomon say of the commandments of God?
   A. Prov. vi. 23.
1. Q. In what spirit do we therefore enter this season?
   A. Distrusting our own thoughts.
2. Q. What do we confess in the Collect?
   A. That through the weakness of our mortal nature we can do no good thing without the help of God.
3. Q. What does St. Paul confess of his inability to do good?
   A. Rom. vii. 18.
4. Q. Is it possible to please God if we yield to the flesh?
   A. Rom. viii. 8.
1. Q. What power, not our own, is given to help our weakness?
   A. The power of the Holy Spirit.
2. Q. How can we obtain this assistance?
   A. By praying that the Holy Spirit may dwell in us.
3. Q. Did our Saviour promise that our prayers for strength should always be answered?
   A. St. Luke xi. 13.
4. Q. Was David's prayer for strength answered?
   A. Ps. cxxxviii. 3.
1. Q. What other love should we have beside our love for God?
   A. We must love one another.

2. Q. What argument does the Epistle use for brotherly love?
A. "If God so loved us, we ought also to love one another."
3. Q. How much did God love us?
A. St. John iii. 16.
4. Q. How are we therefore expected to treat our brethren?
A. Eph. iv. 32.
1. Q. Is it possible to love God and hate our brother
A. No; the Epistle says that such an one professing to love God is a liar.
2. Q. Who is meant by our brother in this connection
A. Every human being, who are our brethren as the sons of our common father Adam.
3. Q. What argument does St. John use to prove that we cannot love God if we hate our brother?
A. 1 St. John iv. 20.
4. Q. What was the Jewish law which Christ abolished?
A. Ex. xxi. 24, 25.
1. Q. What story did our Saviour relate to illustrate this truth?
A. The story of the Rich-man and Lazarus.
2. Q. What became of both of these men?
A. They both alike died and were buried.
3. Q. Where was the beggar Lazarus carried?
A. St. Luke xvi. 22.
4. Q. What did Abraham answer the Rich-man when he asked to be relieved of his torment?

A. St. Luke xvi. 25.
1. Q. What did the Rich-man do?
A. He did nothing, and therefore the beggar starved at his gate.
2. Q. What does this teach us?
A. That we may sin against our brethren by omission as well as by acts of unkindness.
3. Q. What does Christ say of omission in duty?
A. St. Matt. xxiii. 23.
4. Q. How far does our Saviour say our love to our neighbour should extend?
A. St. Matt. v. 44.

> "O love divine, how sweet thou art!
> When shall I find my willing heart
>   All taken up in Thee?
> I thirst, I faint, I die to prove
> The greatness of redeeming love,
>   The love of Christ to me."
>
> *Wesley.*

THE SECOND SUNDAY AFTER TRINITY.

The Collect.

O LORD, who never failest to help and govern those whom thou dost bring up in thy steadfast fear and love; Keep us, we beseech thee, under the protection of thy good providence, and make us to have a perpetual fear and love of thy holy Name; through JESUS CHRIST our Lord. *Amen.*

The Epistle. 1 St. John iii. 13.—*The Gospel.* St. Luke xiv. 16.

1. Q. What are we taught in the Collect for this day?
A. That God helps us to love and fear him.
2. Q. What do you mean by fearing God?

A. Dreading lest we offend him by our sins.
3. Q. What does David say that God will be to those who fear him?
A. Ps. xxv. 12.
4. Q. What will be the result of godly fear in our hearts?
A. Jer. xxxii. 40.
1. Q. What are we again reminded will follow our love to God?
A. Love to our neighbours.
2. Q. How are we instructed to show our love to our neighbours?
A. By ministering to their necessities.
3. Q. How does the Apostle say we should love each other?
A. 1 St. John iii. 18.
4. Q. What is the commandment which God has given us?
A. 1 John iii. 23.
1. Q. Of what do we read in the gospel?
A. Of a great supper which a certain man made.
2. Q. What is this feast designed to represent?
A. The feast of good things spread out for us in the gospel.
3. Q. To what does our Saviour liken a marriage feast?
A. St. Matt. xxii. 2.
4. Q. When does Isaiah say that such a feast shall be prepared for God's people?
A. Isaiah xxv. 6.

1. Q. What did he send his servant to tell those that were invited?
   A. "Come; for all things are now ready."
2. Q. Who are sent to invite men to the heavenly feast?
   A. Those who are divinely ordained to preach the gospel.
3. Q. Who were sent before the time of Christ?
   A. Jer. xxv. 4.
4. Q. What does Isaiah prophecy in reference to the gospel feast?
   A. Isaiah lv. 1.
1. Q. Did all those who were invited come to this feast?
   A. No; they all made excuses.
2. Q. What is this like in the Spiritual world?
   A. The disposition of men to refuse the offers of salvation.
3. Q. What assurance have we that our earthly welfare will not suffer by our accepting God's invitation?
   A. St. Matt. vi. 33.
4. Q. What will be the result of our refusal?
   A. Prov. i. 24–27.
1. Q. What did the master of the house do when he heard of the refusal of those who were invited?
   A. He sent out for the poor, the halt, the lame and the blind.
2. Q. To what has this parable reference?

A. To the calling of the Jews, and afterwards the Gentiles, showing the willingness of the Gentiles to accept the gospel while the Jews refused.

3. Q. What did St. Paul say to those Jews who refused to listen to him?

A. Acts xiii. 46.

4. Q. Are we led to suppose that the Jews will eventually be brought into the fold of Christ?

A. Rom. xi. 25, 26.

1. Q. What again did the master command his servants to do?

A. To go into the highways and hedges and compel them to come in.

2. Q. What duty does this teach us?

A. To go into the lowest places to seek and save those that are lost.

3. Q. How do we know that the gospel is meant for all men?

A. Col. iii. 11.

4. Q. Where were the Apostles commanded to go and preach?

A. St. Mark xvi. 15.

1. Q. What did Christ say of those who were first invited?

A. They should not taste of his supper.

2. Q. What will happen if we do not accept the invitations of the gospel?

A. We shall not taste of the joys of heaven.

3. Q. Are we commanded to accept of it early in life
A. Eccles. xii. 1.
4. Q. What danger do we run in refusing the gospel invitation?
A. Heb. xii. 25.

"—— Who loves the Lord aright,
  No soul of man can worthless find;
All will be precious in his sight,
  Since Christ on all hath shin'd,
But chiefly Christian souls; for they,
Though worn and soiled with sinful clay,
Are yet, to eyes that see them true,
All glistening with baptismal dew."

Keble.

THE THIRD SUNDAY AFTER TRINITY.

The Collect.

O LORD, we beseech thee mercifully to hear us; and grant that we, to whom thou hast given an hearty desire to pray, may, by thy mighty aid, be defended and comforted in all dangers and adversities, through JESUS CHRIST our Lord. Amen.

The Epistle. 1 St. Peter v. 5.—*The Gospel.* St. Luke xv. 1.

1. Q. What is the great truth of this day?
A. That God is merciful to sinners.
2. Q. To whom is the mercy of God extended?
A. To all who call upon Him faithfully.
3. Q. What does David say of God's merciful disposition?
A. Ps. cxlv. 18.
4. Q. Are we called upon to praise God for His mercy?

A. Ps. lix. 16.
1. Q. How did our blessed Lord show His mercy to publicans and sinners?
A. He allowed them to come near to hear Him.
2. Q. Were publicans regarded as being as bad as sinners?
A. They were tax-collectors, who were looked upon by the Jews as great offenders.
3. Q. How did our Saviour express His approbation of the prayer of a publican?
A. St. Luke xviii. 14.
4. Q. Was there a publican among the Apostles of Christ?
A. St. Matt. x. 3.
1. Q. How did the Scribes and Pharisees behave, when they saw the publicans and sinners approaching Christ?
A. They found fault with Him for eating with sinners.
2. Q. What did Christ show by His action?
A. That He is willing to receive all sinners who come to Him in penitence.
3. Q. How does God show His desire to pardon sinners?
A. Ezek. xxxiii. 11.
4. Q. In what way did God manifest His love for sinners?
A. Rom. v. 8.
1. Q. What did Christ show in the parable of the Gospel?

A. That He came to save the lost sheep.
2. Q. Who are the lost sheep?
A. All those who do not love the Lord.
3. Q. Where is Christ called a shepherd?
A. St. John x. 11.
4. Q. Where are we likened to sheep?
A. Isai. liii. 6.
1. Q. What does Christ say of the joy in heaven?
A. That the conversion of one sinner would cause joy in heaven.
2. Q. What is meant by the conversion of a sinner?
A. His repentance and forsaking of his sins.
3. Q. What song is sung in heaven to Christ for this work of redemption?
A. Rev. v. 9.
4. Q. Will there be many who will be redeemed by Christ?
A. Rev. vii. 9.
1. Q. How in another parable did Christ show his interest in the sinner?
A. By showing the joy of the woman who found her piece of silver.
2. Q. What did the rejoicing of her neighbours signify?
A. The joy of the angels over the redeemed.
3. Q. Are the angels said to be interested in the salvation of men?
A. Heb. i. 14.
4. Q. Does God delight in our repentance?
A. Ezek. xviii. 23.
1. Q. Who is it that leads the sheep of Christ astray?

A. The Devil.
2. Q. What other names are given to him in the Bible
A. Satan, the Dragon, the Tempter, Beelzebub the wicked one, the Serpent, &c.
3. Q. What does St. Peter say is the Devil's way of entrapping the sinner?
A. 1 St. Pet. v. 8.
4. Q. Was our blessed Lord ever tempted of the Devil?
A. St. Matt. iv. 1.
1. Q. What are we called upon to do therefore?
A. To be sober and watchful.
2. Q. How are we to fight against Satan?
A. By employing the grace which God has given us in the holy sacraments for our defence and assistance.
3. Q. If we persistently resist the temptations of Satan, will we finally conquer him?
A. St. Jas. iv. 7.
4. Q. How does St. Paul tell us to resist the Devil?
A. Eph. vi. 11.

" O turn, and be thou turn'd! the selfish tear,
　In bitter thoughts of low-born care begun,
Let it flow on, but flow refined and clear,
　The turbid waters, brightening as they run.

O lost and found! all gentle souls below
　Their dearest welcome shall prepare, and prove
Such joy o'er thee, as raptured Seraphs know,
　Who learned their lesson at the Throne of Love."
Keble.

THE FOURTH SUNDAY AFTER TRINITY
The Collect.

O GOD, the protector of all that trust in thee, without whom nothing is strong, nothing is holy; Increase and multiply upon us thy mercy; that thou being our ruler and guide, we may so pass through things temporal, that we finally lose not the things eternal: grant this, O heavenly FATHER, for JESUS CHRIST'S sake our Lord. *Amen.*

The Epistle. Rom. viii. 18.—*The Gospel.* St. Luke vi. 36.

1. Q. What do we learn from the mercy which God shows us?
  A. That we should also be merciful to each other.
2. Q. To whom should our mercy be extended?
  A. Not only to our friends and acquaintances, but even to our enemies.
3. Q. By what prayer did Christ show mercy to His enemies?
  A. St. Luke xxiii. 34.
4. Q. What promise is extended to those who show mercy?
  A. St. Matt. v. 7.
1. Q. In what way are we to be merciful?
  A. By not judging or condemning others.
2. Q. What does this mercy include?
  A. A disposition to forgive any wrong done to us.
3. Q. What depends upon our forgiveness of our enemies?
  A. St. Matt. vi. 14, 15.
4. Q. Who is it that shall have power to judge?

A. 1 Cor. iv. 5.
1. Q. What else is included in the idea of mercy to others?
   A. That we should give to those who need.
2. Q. How much did the law require the Jews to give?
   A. One tenth of all they possessed; which law Christ did not repeal.
3. Q. What example of benevolence did our Saviour commend?
   A. St. Luke xix. 8.
4. Q. What measure of reward is promised to those who give to the Lord?
   A. St. Mark iv. 24.
1. Q. How does Christ show in the parable, the folly of sinners judging sinners?
   A. By showing that the blind cannot lead the blind.
2. Q. Who among the Jews did our Lord call blind leaders?
   A. The Pharisees who were always judging others.
3. Q. Did Christ appoint leaders or guides in His Church whom we should respect?
   A. Heb. xiii. 7.
4. Q. Who above all should we look to as our leader and guide?
   A. Ps. xlviii. 14.
1. Q. What are we to strive to become?
   A. To become perfect like our Lord?
2. Q. What do you mean by being perfect?

THE FOURTH SUNDAY AFTER TRINITY.

 A. Possessing that religious spirit which shall be made perfect in heaven.
3. Q. Are we expected to be like unto Christ?
 A. 1 St. Pet. ii. 21.
4. Q. May we hope to be more like Christ if we follow His blessed steps?
 A. 1 St. John iii. 2.
1. Q. What does the Collect say of our perfection?
 A. That "nothing is strong, nothing is holy."
2. Q. From what source do we derive our strength and goodness?
 A. From God, through the influence of His Holy Spirit.
3. Q. Can any one be as holy as God?
 A. 1 Sam. ii. 2.
4. Q. Where is God spoken of as the giver of strength?
 A. Ps. lxviii. 35.
1. Q. What do we pray that we may pass through?
 A. Things temporal.
2. Q. What do you mean by things temporal?
 A. The events and temptations, which occur in our life-time.
3. Q. What great event makes these temporal things of but little value?
 A. Ps. lxxv. 3.
4. Q. What is said of earthly things in comparison of heavenly?
 A. St. Matt. vi. 19, 20.
1. Q. To what does the Christian hope to be brought at last?

 A. To enjoy the "things eternal."
2. Q. What are these "things eternal?"
 A. Those joys and pleasures which Christ has prepared for those who love Him, in heaven.
3. Q. What does Christ say to those who do not employ their earthly treasures aright?
 A. Q. St. Luke xvi. 11.
4. Q. To what inheritance are the faithful encouraged to look forward?
 A. 1 St. Pet. i. 4.

" He bids us hear, at each sweet pause,
 From care, and want, and toil,—
When dewy eve her curtain draws
 Over the day's turmoil.

In the low chant of wakeful birds,
 In the deep weltering flood,
In whispering leaves, these solemn words,—
 ' God made us all for good.' "

Keble.

THE FIFTH SUNDAY AFTER TRINITY.
The Collect.

GRANT, O LORD, we beseech thee, that the course of this world may be so peaceably ordered by thy governance, that thy Church may joyfully serve thee in all godly quietness, through JESUS CHRIST our Lord. *Amen.*

The Epistle. 1. St. Peter iii. 8.—*The Gospel.* St. Luke v. 1.

1. Q. What do we pray for in the Collect of this day?
 A. The peace and prosperity of Christ's Church.
2. Q. Why do we pray for this peace?

A. Because men are often deprived of opportunities of public worship through the malice of ungodly men.

3. Q. How did Manasseh profane God's house?
A. 2 Chron. xxxiii. 7.

4. Q. Did our Saviour find that men were profaning God's holy Temple?
A. St. Matt. xxi. 12, 13.

1. Q. What is the Church of Christ?
A. It is the visible organization which He established on earth.

2. Q. Is *any* religious organization properly the Church of Christ?
A. To be a true Church it must have its divinely appointed ministry besides the Word and the Sacraments.

3. Q. What happened to Korah for attempting to establish a Church without this divine ordination?
A. Num. xvi. 32.

4. Q. What does this teach us of all merely human organizations?
A. Ps. cxxvii. 1.

1. Q. What is meant by the prayer for "Christ's Church militant?"
A. A prayer for the Church carrying on a Spiritual warfare against the world.

2. Q. Why is it called militant?
A. Because of its warfare against the enemies of our souls.

3. Q. Where are we taught to pray for Christ's Church?
A. Ps. cxxii. 6.
4. Q. What prayer did Christ offer for the unity of the Church?
A. St. John xvii. 21.
1. Q. Who are members of the Church of Christ?
A. All those who have been baptized.
2. Q. Does baptism make people good Christians?
A. It gives them God's Holy Spirit, and makes them God's children, but if they are unfaithful they are bad children, and will not be acknowledged by him.
3. Q. In what way does St. Peter say that baptism saves us?
A. 1 St. Peter iii. 21.
4. Q. How do we know that even though we be within the covenant we still may perish?
A. St. Luke xiii. 5.
1. Q. What are the ministers of Christ called in the gospel?
A. "Fishers of men."
2. Q. By what titles are the ministers of Christ now known?
A. By the titles of Bishops, Priests, and Deacons.
3. Q. What does St. Paul say of the three orders of the ministry?
A. 1 Cor. xii. 28.
4. Q. Where does he address the officers of the Church in their respective orders?

A. Phil. i. 1.
1. Q. Who are to be brought into the Church of Christ?
   A. All the nations of the world.
2. Q. Is the gospel preached in all parts of the known world now?
   A. There are some places where the people have never heard of God.
3. Q. Is the universal spread of the gospel foretold?
   A. Isaiah lii. 10.
4. Q. What prophecy is contained in St. Luke?
   A. St. Luke iii. 6.
1. Q. What other Church do we read of besides the Church militant?
   A. The Church Triumphant?
2. Q. What is the Church Triumphant?
   A. The Church in heaven, where Christ sits on the right hand of God.
3. Q. When will the Church be triumphant?
   A. Rev. xii. 10.
4. Q. When had this final triumph of Christ and his Church been predicted?
   A. Rom. xvi. 20.
1. Q. Will all who belong to the Church militant be included in the Church triumphant?
   A. Only those who are faithful to their baptismal vows.
2. Q. Where will those who are unfaithful be sent?
   A. Into everlasting punishment.
3. Q. Where is the condemnation of the wicked recorded?

A. Ps. ix. 17.
4. Q. How did our Saviour say that good Christians could be distinguished from the bad?
A. St. Matt. vii. 20.

"Head of the hosts in glory!
We joyfully adore Thee,
Thy Church below,
Blending with those on high—
Where through the azure sky
Thy saints in ecstasy
Forever glow!"

Brydges.

THE SIXTH SUNDAY AFTER TRINITY.
The Collect.

O GOD, who hast prepared for those who love thee such good things as pass man's understanding; Pour into our hearts such love toward thee, that we, loving thee above all things, may obtain thy promises, which exceed all that we can desire; through Jesus Christ our Lord. *Amen.*

The Epistle. Rom. vi. 3.—*The Gospel.* St. Matt. v. 20.

1. Q. What are prepared for those who love God?
   A. "Such good things as pass man's understanding."
2. Q. What are these good things beyond our comprehension?
   A. The blessings of religion in this world, and eternal happiness in the world to come.
3. Q. What does St. Paul say of the rewards of loving God?
   A. 1 Cor. ii. 9.

4. Q. What benediction is pronounced upon those who are faithful to their covenant vows?
A. Phil. iv. 7.
1. Q. In what way are we brought within this covenant of grace?
A. By the holy Sacrament of baptism.
2. Q. What do you mean by a Sacrament?
A. "An outward and visible sign of an inward and spiritual grace given unto us; ordained by Christ himself as a means whereby we receive the same, and a pledge to assure us thereof."
3. Q. Did our Saviour make baptism a necessity?
A. St. John iii. 5.
4. Q. How does St. Peter interpret the use of baptism as a means of grace?
A. Acts ii. 38.
1. Q. Into what were we baptized?
A. Into the death of Jesus Christ.
2. Q. What does this mean?
A. That in baptism our sins are buried, having died unto sin.
3. Q. Where is this death in baptism regarded as a token of forgiveness?
A. Col. ii. 13.
4. Q. As salvation depends on "death to sin" how is baptism shown to be this "death to sin?"
A. St. Mark xvi. 16.
1. Q. If we be dead with Christ in baptism what will follow?

A. We shall also live with him.
2. Q. To what life does this refer?
A. To the life everlasting, after the resurrection.
3. Q. How is this parallel of our burial carried into the resurrection of Christ?
A. Rom. vi. 5.
4. Q. Does this resurrection include our bodies as well as our souls?
A. Rom. viii. 11.
1. Q. How should we who are baptized live therefore?
A. In newness of life.
2. Q. What is living in newness of life?
A. As our old life was a life of sin, newness of life is a life of holiness.
3. Q. What is the fruit which we should expect from those who are freed from sin?
A. Rom. vi. 22.
4. Q. If we are holy what must we present unto the Lord?
A. Rom. xii. 1.
1. Q. How holy should we be?
A. Our righteousness should be more than that of the Scribes and Pharisees.
2. Q. What was the righteousness of the Scribes and Pharisees.
A. It was external and formal and did not proceed from the heart.
3. Q. How does our Saviour describe the character of the Scribes and Pharisees?

A. St. Matt. xxiii. 14, 15.
4. Q. How should we serve God?
A. Deut. xxvi. 16.
1. Q. What does our Lord include among great sins?
A. Being angry with our brother.
2. Q. Who is meant by our brother in this connection?
A. All men of whatever nation or condition.
3. Q. Is it right to be angry under any circumstances or at any time?
A. Eph. iv. 26.
4. Q. What is said of him who hateth his brother?
A. 1 St. John iii. 15.
1. Q. What directions did Christ give to those who came to the altar?
A. That before offering their gifts they should be reconciled with all men.
2. Q. Is it wrong to come to the Holy Communion if we are angry with any one?
A. Yes; we must be in love and charity with all men.
3. Q. What did the Jews offer upon their altar?
A. Ex. xxix. 38.
4. Q. Why are we not expected to offer up the same kind of sacrifice?
A. Heb. x. 12.

"Wouldst thou the pangs of gilt assuage?
Lo here an open page,
Where heavenly mercy shines as free,
Written in balm, sad heart, for thee.

Never so fast, in silent April shower,
Flush'd into green the dry and leafless bower,
As Israel's crowned mourner felt
The dull hard stone within him melt."

Keble.

THE SEVENTH SUNDAY AFTER TRINITY.

The Collect.

LORD of all power and might, who art the author and giver of all good things; graft in our hearts the love of thy name, increase in us true religion, nourish us with all goodness, and of thy great mercy keep us in the same, through JESUS CHRIST our Lord. Amen.

The Epistle. Rom. vi. 19.—*The Gospel.* St. Mark viii. 1.

1. Q. What divine attribute do we acknowledge in the Collect?
   A. The omnipotence of God.
2. Q. How is He all-powerful and almighty?
   A. He is able to do any thing that He chooses.
3. Q. Where do you find one of the proofs of God's omnipotence?
   A. 1 Chron. xxix. 12.
4. Q. To whom is all power given in heaven and earth?
   A. St. Matt. xxviii. 18.
1. Q. What proceedeth from God?
   A. All good things; every thing that we have.
2. Q. What do these good things include?
   A. All that we enjoy on earth and all that we hope for in heaven.

THE SEVENTH SUNDAY AFTER TRINITY.

3. Q. What does St. James say of the source of all good gifts?
   A. St. Jas. i. 17.
4. Q. Can we receive nothing except as a gift from God?
   A. St. John iii. 27.
1. Q. What do you pray for in the Collect?
   A. That God "will graft in our hearts the love of His name."
2. Q. If His love is grafted into us, what will it do?
   A. It will become part of our nature and prevent us from sin.
3. Q. What does St. Paul say of the Gentiles being grafted into Christ?
   A. Rom. xi. 23.
4. Q. What does St. John say of those who love God?
   A. 1 St. John iv. 7.
1. Q. What will the love of God increase in us?
   A. True religion and all goodness.
2. Q. What is true religion?
   A. It is a true faith, freedom from sin and faithful practice.
3. Q. How must we worship God?
   A. St. John iv. 24.
4. Q. Is an external and formal worship pleasing to God?
   A. St. Matt. xv. 8, 9.
1. Q. What is related in the gospel?
   A. The miraculous feeding of a great multitude.

2. Q. What does this feeding signify in a spiritual sense?
A. The nourishment of the soul with heavenly food.
3. Q. What example can you give of the compassion which Christ felt for the bodily infirmities of men?
A. St. Matt. xx. 34.
4. Q. What reason did St. Paul give for the ability of Christ to compassionate man in his spiritual infirmities?
A. Heb. v. 2.
1. Q. Did the disciples understand that Christ could satisfy the hunger of the multitude?
A. No; for they asked Him, how they were to be satisfied.
2. Q. What feast did Christ prepare for those who hungered in spirit?
A. The Eucharist, good gift or Holy Communion.
3. Q. Had God ever fed the Jews miraculously before this?
A. Deut. viii. 16.
4. Q. How did God feed Elijah in the wilderness?
A. 1 Kings xvii. 4.
1. Q. What did Christ do before distributing the food?
A. He gave thanks to God for it.
2. Q. What should this teach us?
A. Our duty of giving thanks before meat.
3. Q. Did the Jews give thanks before eating?
A. 1 Sam. ix. 13.

4. Q. Why should we thank God for our daily food?
A. Ps. cxlv. 15.
1. Q. What food does Christ exhort us to seek after?
A. That food which will endure forever.
2. Q. Who is called the bread of life?
A. Jesus Christ, of whom, if we partake, we shall never hunger.
3. Q. By what nourishment are we spiritually fed?
A. St. Matt. iv. 4.
4. Q. Where are we promised that we shall again eat with Christ?
A. St. Luke xiv. 15.

"Bread of heaven, on Thee I feed,
For Thy flesh is meat indeed,
Ever may my soul be fed,
With the true and living Bread:
Day by day with strength supplied,
Through the life of Him who died."

THE EIGHTH SUNDAY AFTER TRINITY.

The Collect.

O GOD, whose never-failing providence ordereth all things both in heaven and earth; We humbly beseech thee to put away from us all hurtful things, and to give us those things which are profitable for us; through Jesus Christ our Lord. *Amen.*

The Epistle. Rom. viii. 12.—*The Gospel.* St. Matt vii. 15.

1. Q. What do we acknowledge in the Collect?
A. That God orders all things in heaven and earth

2. Q. How does God order all things?
A. By caring for, watching over and directing all things for our good.
3. Q. Where do you find the Scripture proof of this truth?
A. 1 Chron. xxix. 12.
4. Q. Has God the knowledge which will enable him thus to order all things?
A. Acts xv. 18.
1. Q. What does this knowledge give us confidence to pray for?
A. That He will preserve us from all hurtful things
2. Q. What are these hurtful things?
A. Whatever may endanger the welfare of our souls.
3. Q. Have we any reason for believing that God will help us?
A. Heb. xiii. 6.
4. Q. How was Christ prepared by His life on earth to understand what assistance we need?
A. Heb. iv. 15.
1. Q. What influence does the Epistle speak of which may hurt our souls?
A. The influence of the flesh.
2. Q. How can the flesh influence us to evil?
A. The flesh is that fallen nature within us, which arouses our evil passions.
3. Q. What does St. Paul say of the influence of the flesh?
A. Gal. v. 17.

4. Q. What does he include among the works of the flesh?
A. Gal. v. 19–21.
1. Q. What other influence does the gospel warn us against?
A. False prophets or teachers.
2. Q. Who are false prophets among us?
A. Those who teach contrary to "the truth as it is in Jesus."
3. Q. Can you give an example of false prophets in the time of the Apostles?
A. 2 Tim. ii. 17, 18.
4. Q. Did St. Peter prophesy that there should be false prophets among us?
A. 2 St. Peter ii. 1.
1. Q. How do these false Prophets appear to us?
A. In sheep's clothing.
2. Q. What does this mean?
A. They appear in a character which does not belong to them.
3. Q. How are false teachers condemned?
A. Gal. i. 8.
4. Q. What did our Saviour say these false prophets would endeavour to do?
A. St. Mark xiii. 22.
1. Q. How can we tell the false from the true teachers?
A. By their fruits.
2. Q. Will they only show it in their conduct?
A. No; they may appear holy while they teach false doctrines.

3. Q. How were the Jews to know a false prophet?
A. Deut. xviii. 22.
4. Q. What fruits will the true teachers bring forth?
A. 2 Tim. ii. 24, 25.
1. Q. What do these false teachers do?
A. They create divisions in the Church and scatter Christ's sheep.
2. Q. What is this division from the Holy Catholic Church called?
A. Schism, which often leads to very great error in faith and practice.
3. Q. Did the Apostle censure the Corinthians for their schism?
A. 1 Cor i. 10.
4. Q. Does he state that schism came through the evil influence of the flesh?
A. 1 Cor. iii. 3.
1. Q. Did Christ design that His Church should be united?
A. Yes; He often spoke of the unity of brethren.
2. Q. Who deplored this Spirit of schism in the Church of Corinth?
A. St. Paul, who saw parties arising, some in the name of Paul, some of Appolo, and some of Cephas.
3. Q. What did he ask them?
A. 1 Cor. i. 13.
4. Q. What sins are apt to follow schism, from which we pray in the Litany to be delivered?

A. "Hardness of heart and contempt of God's word and commandment."

> "One sole baptismal sign,
>   One Lord, below, above,
> Zion, one faith is thine,
>   The only watchword, Love;
> From many temples though it rise,
> One song ascending to the skies.
>
> Head of the Church beneath,
>   The Catholic, the true,
> On all her members breathe,
>   Her broken frame renew!
> Thus shall Thy perfect will be done,
> When Christians love and live as one."
>
> *Robinson.*

THE NINTH SUNDAY AFTER TRINITY.

The Collect.

GRANT to us, Lord, we beseech thee, the spirit to think and do always such things as are right; that we, who cannot do any thing that is good without thee, may by thee be enabled to live according to thy will; through Jesus Christ our Lord. *Amen.*

The Epistle. 1 Cor. x. 1.—*The Gospel.* St. Luke. xvi. 1.

1. Q. What are we taught in the Collect to-day?
   A. That in order to do right we must think right.
2. Q. How do our thoughts affect our actions?
   A. Unless we think and desire to do good we cannot perform good deeds.
3. Q. Where is a willing heart regarded as the beginning of good action?

A. 1 Chron. xxviii. 9.
4. Q. Why should we pray for strength to perform those things which we desire to do?
A. Rom. vii. 18.
1. Q. How must we govern our thoughts?
A. So as to be in accordance with his will.
2. Q. Does God reveal his will in order that we may conform to it?
A. He has revealed his will in the Holy Bible, so that none need mistake it.
3. Q. Who gives us strength to will or desire that which is right?
A. Phil. ii. 13.
4. Q. Is it possible for us to think any thing that is good without God's help?
A. 2 Cor. iii. 5.
1. Q. What do we read in the Epistle?
A. That the Jews did not have a desire to please God.
2. Q. In what way did they show this?
A. By constantly disobeying his commands.
3. Q. Did they receive God's strength to perform their duty?
A. 1 Cor. x. 2, 3, 4.
4. Q. What did our Saviour say would follow our good desire to love and please him?
A. St. John xv. 14.
1. Q. Against what does this history of the Jews warn us?
A. The danger of disobeying God.

THE NINTH SUNDAY AFTER TRINITY.

2. Q. What happened to the Jews on account of this disobedience?
A. They were overthrown in the wilderness.
3. Q. Did our Saviour hold this up as an example to us?
A. 1 Cor. x. 11.
4. Q. What will happen to the children of disobedience?
A. Eph. v. 6.
1. Q. Who are warned to take care lest they fall?
A. Those who think they are standing.
2. Q. What does this show us?
A. That even the holiest among us are liable to fall into sin.
3. Q. Does David acknowledge his liability to fall?
A. Ps. cxliii. 7.
4. Q. How does St. Paul confess his frailty?
A. Rom. vii. 15.
1. Q. What does the gospel teach us?
A. That we are accountable to God for his gifts.
2. Q. What gifts are included in this obligation?
A. Every gift, whether temporal or spiritual.
3. Q. What is required of the stewards of God?
A. 1 Cor. iv. 2.
4. Q. Have each one of us to give account to God for his gifts to us?
A. Rom. xiv. 12.
1. Q. What did the unjust steward do?
A. He acted dishonestly with his master's goods.

2. Q. How may we act dishonestly with the gifts of God?
  A. By squandering them for our own gratification and not using them for his glory.
3. Q. What example of dishonesty was punished by the Apostles?
  A. Acts v. 1, 2.
4. Q. What befell Gehazi for his dishonesty?
  A. 2 Kings v. 27.
1. Q. Are you a steward of Christ?
  A. Yes; of the gifts which He has given me to use for his glory.
2. Q. In what way can you be a good steward?
  A. By devoting my life and all that I have to Christ.
3. Q. When should you begin to serve God as his steward?
  A. Eccles. xii. 1.
4. Q. What reward did our Lord pronounce upon the faithful steward?
  A. St. Matt. xxv. 21.

"Teach me, my God and king,
  Thy will in all to see;
And what I do in any thing,
  To do it as for Thee.

If done beneath Thy laws,
  E'en servile labours shine;
Hallow'd is toil, if Thine the cause;
  The meanest work, divine."

Herbert.

THE TENTH SUNDAY AFTER TRINITY.
The Collect.

LET thy merciful ears, O Lord, be open to the prayers of thy humble servants; and that they may obtain their petitions make them to ask such things as shall please thee; through Jesus Christ our Lord. Amen.

The Epistle. 1 Cor. xii. 1.—*The Gospel.* St. Luke xix. 41.

1. Q. What mercy do we ask for in the Collect?
   A. That God will listen to our prayers.
2. Q. Will our Heavenly Father listen to our prayers?
   A. If we ask Him aright His ears are always open.
3. Q. Under what obligations are we to pray?
   A. St. Luke xviii. 1.
4. Q. What encouragement did Christ give us to pray?
   A. St. Luke xi. 9.
1. Q. What is our first duty in prayer?
   A. To confess our sins.
2. Q. What is included in a proper confession of sin?
   A. A sorrow for sin which will incite us to repentance.
3. Q. What was the first thing that the prodigal Son did on coming back to His Father?
   A. St. Luke xv. 21.
4. Q. How is the duty of confessing our sins shown in the prayer of David?
   A. Ps. xxxii. 5.
1. Q. What must we feel if we would be forgiven of our sins?

16*

A. A hatred for sin which displeases God.
2. Q. How can we show our hatred of sin?
A. By constantly watching and quickly fleeing from the temptation to sin.
3. Q. Are any of us entirely free from sin?
A. 1 St. John i. 8.
4. Q. Is it our duty to watch against sin and its temptations?
A. St. Luke xxi. 36.
1. Q. After confessing those sins which we hate, what are we prepared to do?
A. To pray to be delivered from evil.
2. Q. What will this desire to be freed from evil inspire?
A. A hearty wish for holiness or obedience to God's will.
3. Q. What motive have we to holiness?
A. Levit. xi. 44.
4. Q. Can we hope to see the Lord unless we arrive at some degree of holiness?
A. Heb. xii. 14.
1. Q. What follows our prayer to be delivered from evil?
A. Our prayer to obtain that which is good for us.
2. Q. What feeling must give life to this prayer to receive good?
A. "A lively sense of feeling of God's goodness in all His benefits."
3. Q. What does David say of the goodness of God?
A. Ps. lxxxiv. 11.

4. Q. What argument for the answer of prayer does our Saviour use?
A. St. Luke xi. 13.
1. Q. What therefore should be included in our prayers?
A. Thanks to God for His mercies and favours.
2. Q. How should our praises be excited?
A. By a deep reverence and joyful sense of the perfections of God.
3. Q. What does the Psalmist call upon all people to do?
A. Ps. lxvii. 3.
4. Q. What are we to remember when we sing praises to God?
A. Ps. ciii. 2.
1. Q. What did our Lord do when He went into the Temple?
A. He cast out the money changers.
2. Q. What should this teach us of the house of God?
A. That the Church of God is not to be used for unhallowed and worldly purposes.
3. Q. What command had been given in reference to God's sanctuary?
A. Levit. xxvi. 2.
4. Q. To what prophecy did our Saviour refer in the gospel?
A. Isai. lvi. 7.
1. Q. What did Christ say that the Church was?
A. It was "the house of prayer?
2. Q. What do we learn from this?

A. That public prayer is as essential as private prayer.
3. Q. Did the early Christians meet often in public worship?
A. Acts ii. 42.
4. Q. What is the highest act of Christian worship?
A. The celebration of the Holy Eucharist or Communion.

"Lord, teach us how to pray aright,
With reverence and with fear;
Though dust and ashes in Thy sight,
We may, we must draw near:
We perish if we cease from prayer,
Oh! grant us power to pray;
And when to meet Thee we prepare,
Lord, meet us by the way."

Montgomery.

THE ELEVENTH SUNDAY AFTER TRINITY.

The Collect.

O GOD, who declarest thy almighty power chiefly in showing mercy and pity; mercifully grant unto us such a measure of thy grace, that we, running the way of thy commandments, may obtain thy gracious promises, and be made partakers of thy heavenly treasure, through JESUS CHRIST our Lord. Amen.

The Epistle. 1 Cor. xv. 1.—*The Gospel.* St. Luke xviii. 9.

1. Q. How is God's power most plainly shown?
A. In His mercy and pity.
2. Q. In what way was the power of our Saviour chiefly shown?

THE ELEVENTH SUNDAY AFTER TRINITY.

A. In using his miraculous power for the relief of misery.

8. Q. How great is God's mercy said to be?
A. Ps. ciii. 17.

4. Q. What instance of God's mercy was given as an evidence of His power?
A. Ps. cvi. 8.

1. Q. How did Christ show His power in mercy to the publican?
A. By receiving his prayer.

2. Q. What is taught us here, as to the Spirit in which we should offer prayer?
A. That we should pray with an humble spirit, conscious of our unworthiness.

3. Q. Did Christ approve of the spirit of the Pharisees?
A. St. Matt. v. 20.

4. Q. Are there any who can plead their own merits in prayer?
A. Tit. iii. 5.

1. Q. Who were the Pharisees?
A. A sect of the Jews who were very strict in obeying the letter of the law.

2. Q. Who were the Publicans?
A. They were tax-collectors, who for their extortions were very generally hated and despised by the Jews.

8. Q. Was it customary for the Jews to say their prayers often in the temple?
A. St. Luke xxiv. 53.

4. Q. What excited hatred against the Publicans, and which Christ reproved them for?
A. St. Luke iii. 13.
1. Q. How did the Pharisee pray?
A. With pride in his heart that he was not like the Publican.
2. Q. What did he say he was free from?
A. Those gross sins which are degrading to humanity.
3. Q. Had God condemned men who indulged in these vices?
A. 1 Cor. vi. 9, 10.
4. Q. What does God say to those who think that they need nothing?
A. Rev. iii. 17, 18.
1. Q. What merit did the Pharisee claim?
A. That he gave a tenth of his goods to God and fasted twice a week.
2. Q. Does the Church appoint any regular weekly fast?
A. "Every Friday in the year except Christmas-day."
3. Q. Were the Pharisees careful to pay their tithes?
A. St. Luke xi. 42.
4. Q. What did our Saviour say of fasting?
A. St. Mark ii. 20.
1. Q. What was the fault in the prayer of the Pharisee?
A. He did not acknowledge his own sinfulness.
2. Q. In what consisted the merit of the Publican?

A. In that he confessed that he was unworthy of the mercy of God.
8. Q. What prayer of David was like this one of the Publican?
A. Ps. li. 1, 2.
4. Q. Of what was smiting oneself indicative?
A. Jer. xxxi. 19.
1. Q. What was Christ's decision in reference to these two prayers?
A. The Publican was justified while the Pharisee was not.
2. Q. What do you mean by being justified?
A. He was accounted righteous.
3. Q. Does God love humble and contrite sinners?
A. Isai. lvii. 15.
4. Q. Can we possibly merit the mercy of God?
A. St. Luke xvii. 10.
1. Q. What therefore must we do in approaching God?
A. We must humble ourselves.
2. Q. How can we humble ourselves?
A. By feeling our unworthiness and the infinite perfection of God.
3. Q. What did our Saviour add in this commendation of the Publican?
A. St. Luke xviii. 14.
4. Q. To whom therefore must we give glory for all the good that we may do?
A. Ps. cxv. 1.

"Pray only that thine aching heart,
From visions vain content to part,
Strong for love's sake its woe to hide
May cheerful wait the cross beside,
Too happy if, that dreadful day,
Thy life be given thee for a prey."

Keble.

THE TWELFTH SUNDAY AFTER TRINITY.
The Collect.

ALMIGHTY and everlasting God, who art always more ready to hear than we to pray, and art wont to give more than either we desire or deserve; Pour down upon us the abundance of thy mercy; forgiving us those things whereof our conscience is afraid, and giving us those *good* things which we are not worthy to ask, but through the merits and mediation of Jesus Christ, thy Son, our Lord. *Amen.*

The Epistle. 2 Cor. iii. 4.—*The Gospel.* St. Mark vii. 31.

1. Q. Is God as willing to hear our prayers as we are to ask?
A. Yes; He is more ready and willing.
2. Q. Are not men always ready to pray for what they need?
A. No; because they think that it is useless to pray.
3. Q. Does God daily show his disposition to have mercy on us?
A. Ps. lxviii. 19.
4. Q. Does Christ promise to answer prayer?
A. St. Matt. vii. 7.
1. Q. How great does the Collect say God's mercies are?

THE TWELFTH SUNDAY AFTER TRINITY.

    A. Greater than we can ask or deserve.
2. Q. Does not man deserve the mercies of God?
    A. By his sin man has forfeited all right to God's mercy.
3. Q. How must we ask for God's mercy?
    A. St. Jas. i. 6.
4. Q. What should men learn from God's goodness?
    A. 1 Tim. vi. 18.
1. Q. What must we always remember in our prayers?
    A. To ask God's forgiveness for our sins.
2. Q. If we ask this in a true spirit what will we feel?
    A. A strong purpose of forsaking sin by God's help.
3. Q. What does Daniel say belongs to God?
    A. Dan. ix. 9.
4. Q. Does our forgiveness depend on our confession of sin?
    A. 1 St. John i. 9.
1. Q. How did Christ show his mercy in the Gospel?
    A. By causing the deaf and dumb man to hear and speak.
2. Q. What did the sigh of our Saviour before healing him signify?
    A. It was an evidence of his human sympathy.
3. Q. What other instances can you mention where our Saviour expressed his sympathy?
    A. St. John xi. 33, 35.
4. Q. What consolation for sinners does St. Paul draw from this human sympathy of our blessed Redeemer?

A. Heb. iv. 15.
1. Q. For the forgiveness of what sins do we especially ask?
A. "Those things of which our conscience is afraid."
2. Q. What are these sins?
A. Those which the Holy Ghost convinces us are deserving of punishment.
3. Q. What does St. John say of sin?
A. 1 St. John v. 17.
4. Q. Is there any sin so great that God will not forgive it?
A. St. Luke xii. 10.
1. Q. How is sin pardoned?
A. Through the sacrifice and death of Jesus Christ.
2. Q. Did Christ give power to his ministers to pronounce the pardon of sinners?
A. Yes; the Priest may declare on the authority of Christ, that true penitent sinners are pardoned.
3. Q. Where did Christ give this authority?
A. St. John xx. 23.
4. Q. How do we know that this power could be conferred by the Apostles to their successors?
A. St. John xx. 21.
1. Q. Can men forgive sins of themselves?
A. No; God only can forgive sins.
2. Q. How then can the Priests of the Church proclaim forgiveness?
A. They declare it in Christ's name, acting for Him.

3. Q. In what part of the Church service is this power used?
A. After each of the confessions.
4. Q. What is it called?
A. "The declaration of absolution or remission of sins."
1. Q. How does the Christian feel when he asks God's forgiveness?
A. As if he hardly dare to ask for His mercy.
2. Q. Why do we feel thus fearful?
A. Because of our unworthiness and sinfulness.
3. Q. Are the merits of Christ sufficient without any merit of our own?
A. 1 St. John i. 7.
4. Q. What does the Apostle therefore conclude?
A. Eph. iii. 12.

"The deaf may hear the Saviour's voice,
  The fetter'd tongue its chains may break;
But the deaf heart, the dumb by choice,
  The laggard soul, that will not wake,
The guilt that scorns to be forgiven;
  These baffle e'en the spells of heaven;
In thought of them his brows benign
  Not even in healing cloudless shine."

Keble.

THE THIRTEENTH SUNDAY AFTER TRINITY.

The Collect.

ALMIGHTY and merciful God, of whose only gift it cometh that thy faithful people do unto thee true and laudable service; Grant, we beseech thee, that we

THIRTEENTH SUNDAY AFTER TRINITY.

may so faithfully serve thee in this life, that we fail not finally to attain thy heavenly promises; through the merits of Jesus Christ our Lord. *Amen.*

The Epistle. Gal. iii. 16.—*The Gospel.* St. Luke x. 23.

1. Q. What did the young man in the gospel wish to know?
A. What to do to inherit eternal life.
2. Q. Where did Christ tell him he could find out?
A. In "the book of the law."
3. Q. What is meant by "the book of the law?"
A. The first five books of the Old Testament.
4. Q. Had God promised salvation to those who were obedient to the law?
A. Ezek. xviii. 27.
1. Q. What does "the law" say that men should do?
A. Love God with all their hearts, and their neighbours as themselves.
2. Q. Is the Christian bound by this law as the Jews?
A. Yes; as the gospel for to-day is designed to show.
3. Q. What induces us to love God?
A. 1 St. John iv. 19.
4. Q. Will love to our neighbour follow our love to God?
A. 1 St. John iv. 20.
1. Q. Did Christ say that this was enough?
A. Yes; He said "This do and thou shalt live."
2. Q. What had our Saviour said before in reference to these laws of love to God and our neighbour?

THIRTEENTH SUNDAY AFTER TRINITY. 197

    A. That on these hung all the law and the Prophets.
3. Q. How many have kept the whole law?
    A. Rom. iii. 23.
4. Q. How then can we live, if we have broken the law?
    A. Gal. iii. 13.
1. Q. What did the young lawyer next ask?
    A. Who was his neighbour?
2. Q. How did Christ reply to him?
    A. By relating the story of the man who fell among thieves.
3. Q. Why did the lawyer ask this question?
    A. St. Luke x. 29.
4. Q. What had the young man probably done which Christ afterwards reproved lawyers in general for doing!
    A. St. Luke xi. 46.
1. Q. Who passed by the wounded man?
    A. A Priest and a Levite.
2. Q. In what consisted their sin?
    A. The omission of rendering him assistance.
3. Q. Where does Christ denounce sins of omission as being violations of the law?
    A. St. Matt. xxv. 45.
4. Q. Did the Priest and Levite violate their own law?
    A. Deut. xv. 11.
1. Q. Who was it that showed compassion to the poor man?

A. A Samaritan?
2. Q. What made the action of the Samaritan more praiseworthy?
A. That the man who fell among thieves was probably a Jew.
3. Q. How did the Jews regard the Samaritans?
A. St. John iv. 9.
4. Q. What was one of the accusations of the Jews against Christ?
A. St. John viii. 48.
1. Q. What did our Saviour ask the young man?
A. Which of them was the true neighbour.
2. Q. What did he answer?
A. That the Samaritan was.
3. Q. On what fact did he base his conclusion?
A. On the fact that the Samaritan showed mercy to the poor man.
4. Q. What did our Saviour tell the young lawyer to do?
A. St. Luke x. 37, last clause.
1. Q. What are we taught in this story?
A. Our duty in showing kindness to our neighbours.
2. Q. How can we do this?
A. By speaking kindly as well as by rendering them all the assistance in our power.
3. Q. Can we keep the law without this charity?
A. 1 St. John iii. 17.
4. Q. What did our Saviour say of benevolence?
A. St. Luke vi. 35.

> "O, may we love each other, Lord,
>   As we are loved of Thee!
> For none are truly born of God,
>   Who live in enmity.
> So shall the vain contentious world
>   Our peaceful lives approve;
> And wondering say, as they of old,
>   'See how these Christians love.'"

THE FOURTEENTH SUNDAY AFTER TRINITY.

The Collect.

ALMIGHTY and everlasting God, give unto us the increase of faith, hope, and charity; and, that we may obtain that which thou dost promise, make us to love that which thou dost command; through Jesus Christ our Lord. *Amen.*

The Epistle. Gal. v. 16.—*The Gospel.* St. Luke xvii. 11.

1. Q. What are we taught in the Collect for to-day?
   A. The necessity of Faith, Hope, and Charity.
2. Q. Are these three virtues inseparable?
   A. Yes; for Faith teaches us while Hope gives us confidence to do what Charity inspires.
3. Q. Who is it that makes these virtues increase or grow?
   A. 1 Cor. iii. 7.
4. Q. How did our Saviour illustrate this truth by the vine and its branches?
   A. St. John xv. 5.
1. Q. What is faith?
   A. A belief in that which God has told us in the Bible.

2. Q. How has the Church collected the chief points of faith?
A. In the Apostles' and Nicene creeds.
3. Q. How does St. Paul describe faith?
A. Heb. xi. 1.
4. Q. What duty are we earnestly exhorted to perform?
A. St. Jude 3.
1. Q. What is hope?
A. Confidence in the blessed promises of Christ.
2. Q. What are these promises?
A. God's gifts and helps in this world, and everlasting life in the world to come.
3. Q. What does Jeremiah say of him whose hope is in the Lord?
A. Jer. xvii. 7.
4. Q. Must we be true Christians in order that our hope will be realized?
A. Job viii. 13.
1. Q. What does the word Charity mean here?
A. Love, which should be the mainspring of all our actions.
2. Q. Cannot we keep God's commandments without loving them?
A. It is very difficult for us to do our duty unless we are impelled by love.
3. Q. What does St. Peter say that Charity will do?
A. 1 St. Peter iv. 8.
4. Q. Which of these three virtues does St. Paul say is the greatest?

FOURTEENTH SUNDAY AFTER TRINITY.

A. 1 Cor. xiii. 13.
1. Q. Who were said to approach our Lord in the gospel?
A. Ten men who were lepers.
2. Q. What does this disease represent?
A. Sin is the shocking leprosy of the Soul.
3. Q. How was leprosy cleansed under the law?
A. Read Levit. xiv. 2–9.
4. Q. How are the diseases of the soul cleansed?
A. 1 St. John i. 7.
1. Q. Did Christ know what was the matter with these men?
A. Yes; as he knows all things.
2. Q. What was our Saviour in the habit of doing?
A. Healing the diseases of men's bodies as well as those of their souls.
3. Q. Does God know all our wants?
A. St. Matt. vi. 8.
4. Q. Does God require us to pray, nevertheless?
A. St. Matt. vii. 7.
1. Q. Why did Christ send these lepers to the Priests?
A. To try their faith.
2. Q. How did this try their faith?
A. Because the law had provided for the cleansing of the leper.
3. Q. Can you give an example where Christ required a sick man to exercise faith before he was cured?
A. St. Mark ii. 11.

4. Q. How did the Prophet Elisha try the faith of Naaman?
A. 2 Kings v. 10.
1. Q. How many of the lepers thanked Christ for his mercy?
A. Only one, and he was a Samaritan.
2. Q. What does this show?
A. The indisposition of man to thank God for his mercies.
3. Q. Did Isaiah recognize the duty of giving thanks to God for his goodness?
A. Isaiah xxxviii. 20.
4. Q. What did Esaias say of the mission of Christ?
A. St. Matt. viii. 17.

"Give to the winds thy fears;
  Hope, and be undismayed;
God hears thy sighs and counts thy tears,
  God shall lift up thy head:
Through waves and clouds and storms,
  He gently clears thy way;
Wait thou his time, so shall this night
  Soon end in joyous day."
Gerhardt.

THE FIFTEENTH SUNDAY AFTER TRINITY.
The Collect.

KEEP, we beseech thee, O LORD, thy Church with thy perpetual mercy: and because the frailty of man without thee cannot but fall, keep us ever by thy help from all things hurtful, and lead us to all things profitable to our salvation, through JESUS CHRIST our Lord. Amen.

The Epistle. Gal. vi. 11.—*The Gospel.* St. Matt. vi. 24.

1. Q. What do we ask God to preserve?
   A. His Church with His mercy.
2. Q. By what name is the Church called in Scripture which proves Christ's love for it?
   A. The Bride of Christ.
3. Q. What does St. Peter say of those who are faithful in His Church?
   A. 1. St. Peter ii. 5.
4. Q. Did Christ promise to be with His Church forever?
   A. St. Matt. xxviii. 20.
1. Q. What is the true Church?
   A. The Church which Christ himself appointed and of which He is the head.
2. Q. What does the 19th article of our religion say the visible Church of Christ is?
   A. "A congregation of faithful men in which the pure Word of God is preached, and the Sacraments duly ministered according to Christ's ordinance."
3. Q. What does St. Paul call the Church?
   A. 1 Tim. iii. 15.
4. Q. What did Christ say of the stability of His Church?
   A. St. Matt. xvi. 18.
1. Q. Who have the right to minister in Christ's Church?
   A. Those who have been ordained according to Christ's appointment.
2. Q. How many orders of ministers are there?

A. Three; Bishops, Priests, and Deacons.
3. Q. How long is it since men presumed to preach without apostolic ordination?
A. About 300 years ago, when some few men denied the necessity of ordination.
4. Q. Who had always ordained the clergy before this time?
A. For 1,500 years after Christ, the Bishops had always ordained the clergy, and no one else pretended to have this power.
1. Q. Will membership of the Church prevent our human weakness?
A. No; we are all weak and liable to fall.
2. Q. What will the frailty of man lead him to do?
A. To commit sin unless prevented by God's grace.
3. Q. Are not the best of us prone to sin?
A. St. Jas. iii. 2.
4. Q. What are we exhorted to do?
A. Gal. v. 1.
1. Q. What therefore do you pray for in the collect?
A. That God will preserve us from all hurtful things.
2. Q. What do you mean by things hurtful?
A. All those things which may pollute the soul and lead us into sin.
3. Q. Is this assistance promised?
A. 2 Thess. iii. 3.
4. Q. How will God preserve those who call on Him for aid?
A. Ps. xxxi. 20.

1. Q. What hurtful thing does our Saviour warn us against in the gospel?
   A. The love of riches.
2. Q. Why cannot we love riches and Christ at the same time?
   A. Because no man can serve two masters.
3. Q. What being alone should we serve and worship?
   A. St. Matt. iv. 10.
4. Q. How did Christ tell us to serve Him?
   A. St. John xii. 26.
1. Q. How did our Saviour express this truth?
   A. "Ye cannot serve God and Mammon."
2. Q. What is Mammon?
   A. A Syriac name for the God of riches.
3. Q. What did our Saviour say of those who trusted in riches?
   A. St. Mark x. 24.
4. Q. What does St. Paul say of the love of riches?
   A. 1 Tim. vi. 10.
1. Q. What then must we first seek?
   A. The kingdom of God and His righteousness.
2. Q. What is promised if we do this?
   A. All that is necessary for our welfare will be given us.
3. Q. What are the rich apt to do?
   A. 1 Tim. vi. 9.
4. Q. What treasures are we told to lay up for ourselves?
   A. St. Matt. vi. 20.

> "Lord, it belongs not to my care,
>   Whether I die or live;
> To love and serve Thee is my share,
>   And this Thy grace must give.
>
> My knowledge of that life is small,
>   The eye of faith is dim;
> But 'tis enough that Christ knows all,
>   And I shall be with Him."
>
> Baxter.

THE SIXTEENTH SUNDAY AFTER TRINITY.
The Collect.

O LORD, we beseech thee, let thy continual pity cleanse and defend thy Church; and, because it cannot continue in safety without thy succour, preserve it evermore by thy help and goodness; through Jesus Christ our Lord. *Amen.*

The Epistle. Ephes. iii. 13.—*The Gospel.* St. Luke vii. 11.

1. Q. What do you mean by God's cleansing His Church?
   A. That all error may be taken from Her and her members.
2. Q. How has error ever crept into the Church?
   A. Through the pride and ignorance of her officers.
3. Q. How does Christ cleanse His Church?
   A. Eph. v. 26.
4. Q. Will God have respect to the people of His ancient, or Jewish Church?
   A. Jer. xxxii. 37, 38.
1. Q. In what should the Church continue steadfast?
   A. In the doctrines of the Bible.
2. Q. How do you know what these doctrines are?

A. They have been settled by the Councils of the Church Catholic.
3. Q. How do we know that we should not interpret the Bible for ourselves?
A. 2 St. Pet. i. 20.
4. Q. How do we know that the Church is the proper interpreter of Scripture?
A. 1 Tim. iii. 15.
1. Q. In what else should we remain steadfast?
A. In the fellowship of the Apostles.
2. Q. What is this fellowship?
A. It is the succession of the ministry through the unbroken line of the Bishops.
3. Q. Where is this fellowship traced back to Christ?
A. 1 St. John i. 3.
4. Q. Did the early Christians remain steadfast in this fellowship?
A. Acts ii. 42.
1. Q. In what practice should the Church be steadfast?
A. In the breaking of bread.
2. Q. To what Sacrament does this refer?
A. The Sacrament of the Lord's Supper, which to the faithful is the bread of life.
3. Q. What does St. John say is the bread of life?
A. St. John vi. 33.
4. Q. What is shown forth in the Sacrament of the Lord's Supper?
A. 1 Cor. xi. 26.
1. Q. How can the Church be preserved in purity?

A. By the Holy Spirit, through prayer.
2. Q. What prayer does this mean?
A. The common united prayer of God's people.
3. Q. What example have we of public prayer?
A. St. Luke i. 10.
4. Q. What prayer did our Saviour leave us which sanctions the use of liturgies?
A. "Our Father which art in heaven," &c.
1. Q. What miracle did Christ work, by which He showed His sympathy for individuals in His Church?
A. He raised the widow's son from the dead.
2. Q. What does this prove?
A. That Christ had the power of God to give life.
3. Q. Why should the wicked fear the resurrection?
A. Dan. xii. 2.
4. Q. Unto what shall we be raised?
A. St. John v. 29.
1. Q. How does Christ show this same mercy now?
A. By raising us from the death of sin.
2. Q. What does this show?
A. That Christ has the power of God to forgive sin.
3. Q. Where is this truth affirmed?
A. Eph. ii. 1.
4. Q. If we rise from sin, shall we die again?
A. Rom. vi. 7–9.
1. Q. What effect had this miracle on the people?
A. To prove that Christ was that true Prophet.
2. Q. What did it cause them to do?

A. To glorify God, and to acknowledge Christ as God.
3. Q. Had they expected this great Prophet?
A. Deut. xviii. 15.
4. Q. What was the prophecy of Zacharias?
A. St. Luke i. 68, 69.

> "The dearest offering we can crave,
>   His portion in our souls to prove,
> What is it to the gift He gave,
>   The only Son of His dear love?
>
> Lovest thou praise? the cross is shame;
>   Or ease? the cross is bitter grief;
> More pangs than tongue or heart can frame
>   Were suffered then without relief."
>
> *Keble.*

THE SEVENTEENTH SUNDAY AFTER TRINITY.

The Collect.

LORD, we pray thee that thy grace may always prevent and follow us, and make us continually to be given to all good works; through Jesus Christ our Lord. *Amen.*

The Epistle. Ephes. iv. 1.—*The Gospel.* St. Luke xiv. 1.

1. Q. How do we ask for the grace of God?
    A. That it may "prevent and follow" us.
2. Q. What does this mean?
    A. That God's grace may "go before us" and keep us steadfast in our purpose.
3. Q. Is this grace of the Spirit necessary?
    A. Heb. xii. 28.
4. Q. May we obtain this grace by asking?

A. Heb. iv. 16.
1. Q. For what purpose do you ask for this grace?
   A. That it may dispose us to good works.
2. Q. Cannot we do any thing that is right without the help of God?
   A. No; one of the Collects tells us we cannot even think what is right without him.
3. Q. What proof have we that God gives us this proper disposition?
   A. Phil. ii. 13.
4. Q. Are we expected to do good works?
   A. Eph. ii. 10.
1. Q. What therefore is necessary for the Christian besides faith?
   A. That he should also be given to good works.
2. Q. Can a person have true faith without works?
   A. No; works are the natural offspring of faith.
3. Q. What does St. James say on this subject?
   A. St. Jas. ii. 26.
4. Q. What does he say of simple faith, which proves that without works it is useless?
   A. St. Jas. ii. 19.
1. Q. What good work of Christ is recorded in the gospel?
   A. The healing of the man who had the dropsy.
2. Q. When was this good work performed?
   A. On the Sabbath.
3. Q. Did the Jews think that it was wrong to heal on the Sabbath day?
   A. St. Luke xiii. 14.

SEVENTEENTH SUNDAY AFTER TRINITY.

4. Q. How did Christ show that there were exceptions in favour of works of mercy on the Sabbath?
A. St. Luke xiv. 5.
1. Q. How must these good works be done?
A. In a spirit of humility.
2. Q. What do you mean by this?
A. We must do our good works, not as if it were a merit in us, but as a duty which we can only imperfectly perform.
3. Q. How does St. Paul tell us to work?
A. Eph. iv. 2.
4. Q. What should make us anxious and careful to do our work well?
A. Eccles. xii. 14.
1. Q. What did our Saviour say we should do when invited to positions of honour?
A. We should take the lowest place.
2. Q. Why should we do this?
A. Because there may be more honourable men invited who deserve to sit above us.
3. Q. What did our blessed Lord say that we should do if we would be exalted?
A. St. Matt. xxiii. 12.
4. Q. What did Christ say to those disciples who desired to be greatest in his kingdom?
A. St. Matt. xx. 27.
1. Q. What one thing are we exhorted to do?
A. To "keep the unity of the Spirit in the bond of peace."

2. Q. How are we to do this?
A. By loving each other, by which we will feel like bearing with each other.
3. Q. How does St. Paul say that we should treat each other?
A. Eph. iv. 32.
4. Q. If we would "keep the bond of peace" what else must we do?
A. Heb. xiii. 17.
1. Q. What "bond" should keep us united?
A. The "one Lord, one faith, one baptism."
2. Q. How are we thus united to Christ?
A. By faith, in baptism we are united to our Lord.
3. Q. Are we all by baptism members of the body of Christ?
A. Rom. xii. 5.
4. Q. Where is the Church called the body of Christ?
A. Col. i. 18.

"Soul, then know thy full salvation,
  Rise o'er sin, and fear, and care;
Joy to find in every station
  Something still to do or bear,
Think what Spirit dwells within thee;
  Think what Father's smiles are thine;
Think that Jesus died to win thee;
  Child of heaven, canst thou repine?"

Lyte.

THE EIGHTEENTH SUNDAY AFTER TRINITY.
The Collect.

LORD, we beseech thee, grant thy people grace to withstand the temptations of the world, the flesh,

EIGHTEENTH SUNDAY AFTER TRINITY.

and the devil; and with pure hearts and minds to follow thee, the only God; through Jesus Christ our Lord. *Amen.*

The Epistle. 1 Cor. i. 4.—*The Gospel.* St. Matt. xxii. 34.

1. Q. What are the three great enemies of the Christian?
   A. "The world, the flesh, and the devil."
2. Q. What did you promise at baptism in reference to them?
   A. "I renounce them all; and by God's help will not follow nor be led by them."
3. Q. What is said of the man who resists these temptations?
   A. St. Jas. i. 12.
4. Q. What are we required to do, in order to successfully resist them?
   A. Eph. vi. 13.

1. Q. How does the world tempt us?
   A. By its allurements and pleasures.
2. Q. What are some of the chief temptations of the world?
   A. Riches, honours, pleasures, and evil companions.
3. Q. What does Christ say of the world?
   A. St. John xv. 19.
4. Q. Are we warned against the danger of loving the world?
   A. 1 St. John ii. 15.

1. Q. What do you understand by the flesh?
   A. Our own corrupt and sinful natures.

2. Q. What are the temptations of the flesh?
A. Sloth, idleness, luxury, indulgence, intemperance in any thing.
3. Q. Against what does the flesh make war?
A. Gal. v. 17.
4. Q. What will those who are Christ's do?
A. Gal. v. 24.
1. Q. Who is the Devil?
A. He is the Spirit of all evil, cast out of heaven for rebellion against God.
2. Q. What does the devil strive to put into our hearts?
A. Pride, malice, envy, unbelief, lying, and all unholy passions.
3. Q. What does St. Peter say the devil does?
A. 1 St. Pet. v. 8.
4. Q. Can these temptations of the devil be successfully resisted?
A. St. Jas. iv. 7.
1. Q. How may all these temptations be resisted?
A. By the grace of God.
2. Q. How is this grace to be obtained?
A. By humbly praying for God's assistance.
3. Q. Will our temptations be greater than we can bear?
A. 1 Cor. x. 13.
4. Q. What spirit must we have in order to obtain this grace?
A. St. Jas. iv. 6.
1. Q. What is our first duty?

EIGHTEENTH SUNDAY AFTER TRINITY.

    A. To love God with all our hearts.
2. Q. What does the Catechism say your duty to God is?
    A. To believe in Him, to fear Him, and to love Him with all my heart, with all my mind, with all my soul, and with all my strength; to worship Him; to give Him thanks; to put my whole trust in Him; to call upon Him; to honour His Holy Name and His Word; and to serve Him truly all the days of my life."
3. Q. Is this law also found in the Jewish Code?
    A. Deut. vi. 5.
4. Q. Why is this the first and great commandment?
    A. 1 St. John iv. 7, 8.
1. Q. What is our second duty?
    A. To love our fellow men.
2. Q. How does the Catechism explain this duty?
    A. "To love him as myself, and to do unto all men as I would they should do unto me; to love, honour, and succour my father and mother; to honour and obey the civil authority; to submit myself to all my governors, teachers, spiritual pastors, and masters; to order myself lowly and reverently to all my betters; to hurt nobody by word or deed; to be true and just in all my dealings; to bear no malice nor hatred in my heart; to keep my hands from picking and stealing, and my tongue from evil speaking, lying, and slandering; to keep my body in temperance, soberness, and

chastity; not to covet nor desire other men's goods; but to learn and labour truly to get mine own living, and to do my duty in that state of life unto which it shall please God to call me."

3. Q. Where in the law is this commandment recorded?
A. Levit. xix. 18.
4. Q. What was our Saviour's rule of action towards our neighbour?
A. St. Matt. vii. 12.
1. Q. What is said of those who truly keep these two commandments?
A. They have fulfilled the law.
2. Q. What does this mean?
A. That they include every virtue which a Christian should possess.
3. Q. Is keeping these commandments better than sacrifice?
A. 1 Sam. xv. 22.
4. Q. Where is this affirmed in the Gospel?
A. St. Mark xii. 33.

"Weak tremblers on the edge of woe,
　Yet shrinking from true bliss,
Our rest must be 'no rest below,'
　And let our prayer be this:
Lord, wave again Thy chast'ning rod,
　Till every idol throne
Crumble to dust, and Thou, O God,
　Reign in our hearts alone."

Keble.

THE NINETEENTH SUNDAY AFTER TRINITY
The Collect.

O GOD, forasmuch as without thee we are not able to please thee; Mercifully grant that thy Holy Spirit may in all things direct and rule our hearts; through Jesus Christ our Lord. *Amen.*

The Epistle. Ephes. iv. 17.—*The Gospel.* St. Matt. ix. 1.

1. Q. Are we able to please God of ourselves?
   A. No; we must be assisted by His grace.
2. Q. What prevents us from pleasing God?
   A. The influence of the world, the flesh and the devil.
3. Q. What does St. Paul say of those who are in the flesh?
   A. Rom. viii. 8.
4. Q. Does Christ say that we can do nothing without Him?
   A. St. John xv. 5.
1. Q. How must we walk so as to please God?
   A. Not as other Gentiles walk.
2. Q. How did these other Gentiles walk?
   A. In the vanity of their minds, being blinded through ignorance.
3. Q. Is ignorance an excuse for sin now?
   A. Acts xvii. 30.
4. Q. Why have we no excuse?
   A. Eph. iv. 20, 21.
1. Q. What is it necessary that we should be?
   A. We must be renewed or born again.

2. Q. How are we first renewed?
   A. By the waters of baptism.
3. Q. How do we know that this new birth refers to baptism.
   A. St. John iii. 5.
4. Q. What action of the Apostles shows that they thus understood the nature of baptism?
   A. Acts ii. 38.
1. Q. What are we guarded against in the Epistle?
   A. The improper use of the tongue?
2. Q. What is it that should alone proceed out of the mouth?
   A. That which is good and profitable to be heard.
3. Q. What does David advise us?
   A. Ps. xxxiv. 13.
4. Q. What does St. James say of him that bridleth not his tongue?
   A. St. Jas. i. 26.
1. Q. What is the best way to prevent evil speaking?
   A. To keep our hearts from anger.
2. Q. What rule is given us in reference to anger?
   A. "Let not the sun go down upon your wrath."
3. Q. What is said of those who permit anger to abide with them?
   A. Eccles. vii. 9.
4. Q. What therefore will the Christian do?
   A. Col. iii. 8.
1. Q. How did Christ prove his ability to bestow grace?
   A. By healing the man sick of the palsy.

2. Q. Of what was this healing typical?
A. Of the power of Christ to forgive sins.
3. Q. How do you know that this is the true interpretation?
A. St. Matt. ix. 5.
4. Q. Where is sin represented under the figure of sickness?
A. Isaiah i. 5, 6.
1. Q. What did the Scribes say of this act of our blessed Lord?
A. That Christ blasphemed.
2. Q. What is blasphemy?
A. Taking God's Holy name in vain, or assuming any of the attributes or powers of God?
3. Q. Why did they think that our Saviour blasphemed in this instance?
A. St. Mark ii. 7.
4. Q. What purpose besides the mercy to the sick man, did Christ have in working this miracle?
A. St. Matt. ix. 6.
1. Q. What effect had this miracle on the multitude?
A. They glorified God that Christ had the power to forgive sins.
2. Q. Did Christ commit this power to His ministers?
A. He gave them power to declare the forgiveness of sins.
3. Q. Where is this power recorded as given to the Apostles?
A. St. John xx. 23.

4. Q. How do we know that the Apostles had the authority to transmit this power?
A. St. John xx. 21.

"I lay my sins on Jesus,
  The spotless Lamb of God,
He bears them all, and frees us
  From the accursed load.
I bring my guilt to Jesus,
  To wash my crimson stains.
White in His blood most precious,
  Till not a spot remains."

Bonar.

THE TWENTIETH SUNDAY AFTER TRINITY.
The Collect.

O ALMIGHTY and most merciful God, of thy bountiful goodness keep us, we beseech thee, from all things that may hurt us; that we, being ready both in body and soul, may cheerfully accomplish those things which thou commandest, through JESUS CHRIST our Lord. Amen.

The Epistle. Ephes. v. 15.—*The Gospel.* St. Matt. xxii. 1.

1. Q. What do we pray for in the Collect?
A. That we may cheerfully do what God commands.
2. Q. How may we do this?
A. By dedicating our souls and bodies to his service.
3. Q. Will a willing mind be accepted even though we do not all that is commanded?
A. 2 Cor. viii. 12.
4. Q. What is said of giving, which will apply to all that we owe to God?

A. 2 Cor. ix. 7.
1. Q. Unto what did Christ liken the kingdom of heaven?
A. To a royal marriage.
2. Q. What is meant here by "the kingdom of heaven?"
A. The place of eternal bliss, to which men are invited.
3. Q. Who is the king here referred to?
A. 1 Tim. vi. 15.
4. Q. Is the beginning of eternal bliss represented by the marriage of Christ?
A. Rev. xix. 7.
1. Q. What did the king command his servants to do?
A. To call them which were bidden or invited.
2. Q. Did all come who were invited?
A. No; many refused to come at all.
3. Q. Whom had God sent unto the Jews to call them to his kingdom?
A. Jer. xxv. 4.
4. Q. What hinders persons from accepting the invitation of God?
A. St. John v. 40.
1. Q. When those who were invited refused to come what did the king do?
A. He sent his servants into the high-ways to invite all they could find.
2. Q. How did the Apostles act upon this command?
A. By inviting the Gentiles, after the Jews had refused to acknowledge Jesus?

3. Q. Where was this command given unto them?
A. St. Mark xvi. 15.
4. Q. How many are now invited to his kingdom?
A. Rev. xxii. 17.
1. Q. What feast did our Saviour institute in his kingdom on earth?
A. The feast of the Holy Eucharist.
2. Q. Who may come to this feast?
A. "All such as are confirmed or are ready and desirous to be confirmed."
3. Q. What is Confirmation?
A. The ratification of our baptismal vows, after we are come to years of discretion.
4. Q. By whom are persons confirmed?
A. By the Bishops, who alone have this authority.
1. Q. When the king came in what did he find?
A. "A man who had not on a wedding garment."
2. Q. What did this action of the man signify?
A. A disregard of the affection and honour of the king.
3. Q. Does God promise to furnish us with the wedding garment?
A. Rev. iii. 5.
4. Q. Was it the custom for kings to present garments to their friends?
A. Esther viii. 15.
1. Q. How should we present ourselves at the Holy Communion?
A. In the wedding garment of purity and humility.

2. Q. What are we exhorted to do before coming to the altar?
A. To examine ourselves, so that we may come "holy and clean, "in the marriage garment required by God in Holy Scripture."
3. Q. Is our *own* righteousness sufficient?
A. Isaiah lxiv. 6.
4. Q. Who is our righteousness?
A. 1 Cor. i. 30.
1. Q. What was done with him who came without a wedding garment?
A. He was cast into outer darkness.
2. Q. What shall happen to him who comes to the Holy Communion unworthily?
A. He will be condemned by God.
3. Q. What is this outer darkness called?
A. St. Matt. xiii. 42.
4. Q. With what kind of people shall he be classed?
A. St. Matt. xxiv. 51.

"Bread of Heaven, on Thee I feed,
For Thy flesh is meat indeed,
Ever may my soul be fed,
With the true and living bread:
Day by day, with strength supplied,
Through the life of Him who died.
Vine of heaven, Thy blood supplies
This blest cup of sacrifice;
'Tis Thy wounds my healing give;
To Thy cross I look and live:
Rooted, grounded, graff'd in Thee,
A living branch O let me be."

THE TWENTY-FIRST SUNDAY AFTER TRINITY.
The Collect.

GRANT, we beseech thee, merciful Lord, to thy faithful people pardon and peace, that they may be cleansed from all their sins, and serve thee with a quiet mind; through Jesus Christ our Lord. *Amen.*

The Epistle. Ephes. vi. 10.—*The Gospel.* St. John iv. 46.

1. Q. Of what are we reminded to-day?
   A. That we are the soldiers of Christ.
2. Q. Why is the sign of the cross put on our foreheads at baptism?
   A. "In token that hereafter we shall not be ashamed to confess the faith of Christ crucified; and manfully to fight under His banner."
3. Q. Of what is St. Timothy charged?
   A. 1 Tim. i. 18.
4. Q. What fight is he told to engage in?
   A. 1 Tim. vi. 12.
1. Q. Against whom do we fight?
   A. Against Satan and his followers.
2. Q. What kind of warfare is this?
   A. A spiritual warfare.
3. Q. What does the Epistle say we fight against?
   A. Eph. vi. 12.
4. Q. Of what should we be careful when fighting against some opinion which we do not approve?

A. Acts v. 39.
1. Q. How are we furnished for the battle?
   A. By the armour which God gives us.
2. Q. How did warriors fight in the days of the Apostles?
   A. In hand to hand conflicts, in which armour was very essential.
3. Q. What is this called in the Epistle?
   A. Eph. vi. 11.
4. Q. What is this armour called elsewhere?
   A. Rom. xiii. 12.
1. Q. What are the weapons of defence which Christ gives us?
   A. The girdle, breastplate, sandals, shield, and helmet.
2. Q. What did these pieces of armour protect?
   A. The loins, the breast, the feet, the heart, and the head.
3. Q. What does the Prophet say of righteousness?
   A. Isaiah xi. 5.
4. Q. What did the angel tell St. Peter to do when he set him free from prison?
   A. Acts xii. 8.
1. Q. What graces do these weapons represent?
   A. Truth, righteousness, the gospel of peace, faith, and salvation.
2. Q. Are these weapons sufficient for our defence?
   A. Yes; if we use them aright.
3. Q. How do we know that this grace is sufficient?
   A. 2 Cor. xii. 9.

4. Q. If we are true sons of God, can we overcome the world?
A. 1 St. John v. 4.
1. Q. What weapon for fighting is given us?
A. The sword of the Spirit.
2. Q. What is this sword of the Spirit?
A. It is the Word of God, or the Holy Bible.
3. Q. What is said of the power of this sword?
A. Heb. iv. 12.
4. Q. Does this also search our hearts and try us?
A. Jer. xvii. 10.
1. Q. What are we to do in our Christian warfare?
A. Be constantly watchful.
2. Q. Why should we be thus watchful?
A. Because the devil is always looking out for opportunities to attack us.
3. Q. Why does St. Peter tell us to watch?
A. 1 St. Pet. v. 8.
4. Q. What other reason did our Saviour give for watching?
A. St. Matt. xxvi. 41.
1. Q. How are we to be strengthened for this battle?
A. By praying to God for His assistance?
2. Q. What is prayer?
A. The earnest, heartfelt invocation of the contrite soul.
3. Q. Will the fervent prayer of the righteous avail any thing?
A. St. Jas. v. 16, last clause.

4. Q. What short direction does St. Paul give concerning prayer?
A. 1 Thess. v. 17.

"Soldiers of Christ arise,
  And put your armour on,
Strong in the strength which God supplies
  Through His Eternal Son.

That having all things done,
  And all your conflicts past,
Ye may behold your victory won,
  And stand complete at last."

THE TWENTY-SECOND SUNDAY AFTER TRINITY.

The Collect.

LORD, we beseech thee to keep thy household the Church in continual godliness; that, through thy protection, it may be free from all adversities, and devoutly given to serve thee in good works, to the glory of thy name, through JESUS CHRIST, our Lord. Amen.

The Epistle. Phil. i. 3.—*The Gospel.* 'St. Matt. xviii. 21.

1. Q. What are we taught in the gospel for to-day?
A. The duty of forgiveness.
2. Q. What did St. Peter ask our Saviour?
A. If he should forgive his brother till seven times.
3. Q. How often did the Jews think that forgiveness was required?
A. Amos i. 3.
4. Q. What is it man's glory to do?
A. Prov. xix. 11.

TWENTY-SECOND SUNDAY AFTER TRINITY.

1. Q. How many times did Christ say we should forgive?
   A. Until seventy times seven.
2. Q. What did He mean by this expression?
   A. That there was no limit to the duty of forgiveness.
3. Q. How do we ask to be forgiven?
   A. St. Luke xi. 4.
4. Q. What great example did our Saviour set us of forgiveness?
   A. St. Luke xxiii. 34.

1. Q. To what did Christ liken the kingdom of heaven?
   A. To the king who took account of his servants.
2. Q. To what does this refer?
   A. To the time when Christ shall judge the world.
3. Q. Where are we told that we must render an account for our deeds?
   A. Rom. xiv. 12.
4. Q. Will all of us need the forgiveness of God at that time?
   A. Ps. cxliii. 2.

1. Q. Whom did the king find among his servants?
   A. One who owed him a large debt that he could not pay.
2. Q. What did the king do?
   A. He commanded him to be sold and all that he had, that payment might be made.
3. Q. What evidence have you that this was a Jewish custom?
   A. 2 Kings iv. i.

4. Q. Did this law of sale extend to the Jews themselves?
A. Levit. xxv. 39.
1. Q. What did this servant do?
A. He prayed the king to be patient with him.
2. Q. Was this request granted?
A. Yes; the king forgave him his debt.
3. Q. What duty does the servant's action show us?
A. Dan. ix. 3.
4. Q. Of what does the king's action assure us?
A. 1 St. John i. 9.
1. Q. How did this servant act when he was released?
A. He went and found a fellow-servant who owed him a debt.
2. Q. What was the amount of this second servant's debt?
A. An hundred pence.
3. Q. How much in our money did this amount to?
A. About fourteen dollars.
4. Q. What was the difference between this and the debt of the first servant?
A. The difference between a talent and a penny, if it was silver, was one hundred times; if it was gold, nearly a million.
1. Q. Did this servant forgive his fellow-servant?
A. No; he cast him into prison until he should pay.
2. Q. Had the fellow-servant asked him to be patient?
A. Yes; in the same way that he had asked the favour of the king.

3. Q. Why was this action peculiarly wicked?
A. St. Matt. xviii. 32.
4. Q. What command of Christ had he violated?
A. St. Matt. vii. 12.
1. Q. What did the king do to that wicked servant?
A. He delivered him to the tormentors until he should pay his debt.
2. Q. What did Christ say that God would do?
A. God will do the same to those who are unforgiving.
3. Q. Where else is this truth affirmed?
A. St. Matt. vi. 15.
4. Q. What does Moses declare of God's disposition to forgive?
A. Ex. xxxiv. 6.

> "Yes, ransomed sinner! would'st thou know
>   How often to forgive,
> How dearly to embrace thy foe,
>   Look where thou hop'st to live;
> When thou hast told those isles of light,
>   And fancied all beyond,
> Whatever owns, in depth or height,
>   Creation's wondrous bond;
> There in their solemn pageant learn
>   Sweet mercy's praise to see:
> Their Lord resign'd them all, to earn
>   The bliss of pardoning thee."
>
> *Keble.*

THE TWENTY-THIRD SUNDAY AFTER TRINITY.
The Collect.

O GOD, our refuge and strength, who art the author of all godliness; Be ready, we beseech thee, to hear the devout prayers of thy Church; and grant that those things which we ask faithfully we may obtain effectually; through Jesus Christ our Lord. *Amen.*

The Epistle. Phil. iii. 17.—*The Gospel.* St. Matt. xxii. 15.

1. Q. What do we call God in the Collect?
   A. Our Refuge.
2. Q. Why is God a refuge?
   A. Because we can flee unto him to shelter us from troubles and trials.
3. Q. What does David call God?
   A. Ps. xlvi. 1.
4. Q. Where does the Prophet refer to our Saviour as a refuge?
   A. Isaiah xxxii. 2.
1. Q. What else do you acknowledge that God is?
   A. Our strength.
2. Q. In what way is He our strength?
   A. He is the source from whom comes our strength to resist temptations and evils.
3. Q. What does David say of the strength which he received from God?
   A. Ps. xxvii. 1.
4. Q. How are we to use this strength when we have received it?
   A. St. Luke xxii. 32.
1. Q. What other name is given to God?
   A. The author of all godliness.
2. Q. What do you mean by this?
   A. That all good qualities and purposes come from and are prompted by God?

3. Q. What does St. Peter say of God?
   A. 2 St. Pet. i. 3.
4. Q. Is it our duty to pray for each other?
   A. St. Jas. v. 16.
1. Q. What do we ask God in the Collect?
   A. To listen to the prayers of his Church.
2. Q. What is meant by the prayers of the Church?
   A. The united or common prayer which we offer him in public worship.
3. Q. Is God near to those who call upon him?
   A. Ps. cxlv. 18.
4. Q. Is He also near to the wicked?
   A. Prov. xv. 29.
1. Q. What kind of prayers should we offer?
   A. Devout prayers, or those which come from the heart.
2. Q. What kind of prayers are offensive to God?
   A. Those which come from the lips while the heart is not in them.
3. Q. How does St. Paul say we should pray?
   A. Eph. vi. 18.
4. Q. Why does God hate prayers which come from the lips, while the heart does not desire an answer?
   A. Prov. xii. 22.
1. Q. In what other spirit are we to pray?
   A. In a spirit of faith.
2. Q. What do you mean by praying in a spirit of faith?

TWENTY-THIRD SUNDAY AFTER TRINITY.

 A. Believing that God will answer our prayers as is best for us.

3. Q. Where is the promise of an answer to prayer in faith?
 A. St. Matt. xxi. 22.

4. Q. What confidence may we place in God's readiness to hear?
 A. 1 St. John v. 14.

"Who shall change our vile body that it may be fashioned like unto his glorious body, according to the working whereby He is able even to subdue all things unto himself."—Phil. iii. 21.

"Heavy and dull this frame of limb and heart,
 Whether slow creeping on cold earth, or borne
On lofty steed, or loftier power, we dart
 O'er wave or field; yet breezes laugh to scorn

Our puny speed, and birds, and clouds in heaven,
 And fish, like living shafts that pierce the main,
And stars that shoot through frozen air at even—
 Who but would follow, might he break his chain!

And thou shalt break it soon; the grovelling worm
 Shall find his wings, and soar as fast and free
As his transfigured Lord, with lightning form
 And snowy vest. Such grace He won for thee,

When from the grave He sprang at dawn of morn,
 And led through boundless air thy conquering road,
Leaving a glorious track, where saints new born
 Might fearless follow to their blest abode."

Keble.

THE TWENTY-FOURTH SUNDAY AFTER TRINITY.
The Collect.

O LORD, we beseech thee, absolve thy people from their offences; that through thy bountiful goodness we may all be delivered from the bands of those sins, which by our frailty we have committed. Grant this, O heavenly Father, for Jesus Christ's sake, our blessed Lord and Saviour. *Amen.*

The Epistle. Col. i. 3.—*The Gospel.* St. Matt. ix. 18.

1. Q. What do you pray for to-day?
   A. To be absolved from sin.
2. Q. What do you mean by absolution?
   A. Being freed from the power of sin and its punishment.
3. Q. What prayer did Solomon offer for Israel?
   A. 1 Kings viii. 50.
4. Q. Will the time come when this prayer will be answered?
   A. Jer. xxxi. 34.

1. Q. Do you pray that the Christian or the sinner may be absolved?
   A. In this place we pray for the absolution of Christians.
2. Q. Are not those who are truly Christians free from sin?
   A. No; we all commit sin, and need constant absolution.
3. Q. What does St. James say of our disposition to sin?

TWENTY-FOURTH SUNDAY AFTER TRINITY.

A. St. Jas. iii. 2.
4. Q. Can any one say that he is clean and pure from sin?
A. Prov. xx. 9.
1. Q. In what, therefore, do we all unite in our public worship?
A. In confessing our sins.
2. Q. What do Christians confess in this part of public worship?
A. That we have gone astray, like lost sheep.
3. Q. What does Solomon say of confession?
A. Prov. xxviii. 13.
4. Q. What above all things should every Christian confess?
A. Phil. ii. 11.
1. Q. Why do Christians sin after they are born again?
A. Because of the frailty of their human nature.
2. Q. What are these sins which the Christian commits called?
A. "Sins of weakness, thoughtlessness, or inadvertency."
3. Q. From what are Christians delivered, and to what are they brought?
A. Rom. viii. 21.
4. Q. Shall we ask God for any thing in vain, if we ask in the name of our adorable Saviour?
A. St. John xvi. 23.
1. Q. What happened to Christ in the gospel?

    A. A woman touched His garment that she might be healed.
2. Q. What disease must Christ heal in us?
    A. The disease of sin.
3. Q. Had this woman tried any other means of cure?
    A. St. Luke viii. 43.
4. Q. What had God commanded in reference to the garments of the Jews?
    A. Num. xv. 38.
1. Q. Why did she touch His garment?
    A. She said to herself, "If I touch Him I shall be healed."
2. Q. What did this woman exhibit by this action?
    A. The greatness of her faith.
3. Q. Where else is faith said to have been the means of cure?
    A. St. Luke xvii. 19.
4. Q. What evidence did the multitude, on a certain occasion, give of their faith?
    A. Acts v. 15.
1. Q. Did Jesus know that some one had touched Him?
    A. Yes; He perceived that virtue had gone out of Him.
2. Q. How did he answer the woman?
    A. "Be of good comfort, thy faith hath made thee whole."
3. Q. How should we come, that the diseases of our souls might be cured?
    A. Heb. x. 22.

4. Q. Will Christ hear all those who come to Him?
  A. St. John vi. 37.
1. Q. What other miracle did our Saviour work?
  A. He raised the Ruler's daughter from the dead.
2. Q. Of what does this resurrection assure us?
  A. Of the power of Christ to raise us from the dead.
3. Q. What other instances are recorded in the gospel of Christ's having raised the dead?
  A. St. Luke vii. 14; St. John xi. 43.
4. Q. Will Christ at some future time call all the dead from their graves?
  A. St. John v. 28.

" Glory to God, in full anthems of joy;
The being He gave us, death cannot destroy;
Sad were the life we must part with to-morrow,
If tears were our birthright, and death were our end;
But Jesus hath cheer'd the dark valley of sorrow,
And bade us, immortal, to heaven ascend.
Lift your glad voices in triumph on high,
Jesus hath risen, and man shall not die."
                                        Ware.

THE TWENTY-FIFTH SUNDAY AFTER TRINITY.
The Collect.

STIR up, we beseech thee, O Lord, the wills of thy faithful people; that they, plenteously bringing forth the fruit of good works, may by thee be plenteously rewarded; through Jesus Christ our Lord. Amen.

The Epistle. Jer. xxiii. 5.—*The Gospel.* St. John vi. 5.

1. Q. What is this Sunday?

A. It is the last Sunday of the Christian year.
2. Q. What Sunday follows this?
A. The first Sunday in Advent.
3. Q. What is said of the Collect, Epistle, and Gospel, in the rubric?
A. That they must be used on the last Sunday of the ecclesiastical year.
4. Q. Suppose that there are less or more than twenty-five Sundays after Trinity?
A. If there are less, the Collect, &c., for those Sundays are omitted—if more, the Sundays after the Epiphany, which were omitted, are to be used.
1. Q. What is taught us in the season of Advent?
A. The Coming of Christ to save and to judge us.
2. Q. How did He first come?
A. He came in great humility.
3. Q. What was the object of His coming?
A. To reconcile God to us, and us to God, by the sacrifice of Himself.
4. Q. How will He come in judgment?
A. In great glory, to reward or punish us, according to our acceptance or rejection of His salvation.
1. Q. What did you learn on Christmas?
A. That Christ was born into the world like any other child.
2. Q. Who were His parents?
A. The blessed Virgin Mary and Joseph.
3. Q. At what place was He born?

A. At Bethlehem of Judea in a manger.

4. Q. What does the Creed say of our Saviour's birth?
A. He "was incarnate by the Holy Ghost of the Virgin Mary."

1. Q. What are we taught on the Epiphany?
A. That Christ came to save the Gentiles as well as the Jews.

2. Q. To whom was He manifested, as representatives of the Gentile world?
A. To the three kings who came from the East.

3. Q. Had the Jews been a peculiar people in the sight of God before the Advent of Christ?
A. Yes; Israel had been chosen from among all the nations of the earth?

4. Q. How does the truth of the Epiphany affect us?
A. We are the Gentiles, and therefore we are thus assured of our salvation through the blood of Christ.

1. Q. What great event transpired on Good Friday?
A. Our blessed Saviour was crucified on that day.

2. Q. Where was He crucified?
A. On a mount called Calvary outside the gates of Jerusalem.

3. Q. Was Christ compelled to die for sinners?
A. No; He voluntarily gave Himself for our redemption.

4. Q. Could not men have been saved without His sacrifice?
A. No; Christ's death alone could satisfy God's wrath against man.

1. Q. Did Christ remain in the grave?
   A. He rose from the dead three days after, on Easter morning.
2. Q. Did He remain long upon earth?
   A. After 40 days He ascended into heaven.
3. Q. Of what does the resurrection of Christ assure us?
   A. That we also shall be raised from the dead.
4. Q. What do we learn from His ascension?
   A. That if we be like Him, we shall ascend and be with Him forever.
1. Q. What was given us on Whitsunday?
   A. The Holy Ghost, the Comforter.
2. Q. What was the Holy Ghost given for?
   A. To assist us in becoming holy and fit for heaven.
3. Q. How were you taught that the Holy Ghost was given?
   A. In Christ's Holy sacraments.
4. Q. Are these sacraments therefore necessary to salvation?
   A. The Catechism tells us, that the Sacraments of Baptism and the Lord's Supper are generally—when they can be had—necessary to salvation.
1. Q. What are you taught on Trinity-Sunday?
   A. That the Father, Son and Holy Ghost, are three persons in one adorable Godhead.
2. Q. Why do you believe in the Father?
   A. Because He created us.
3. Q. What reason have you for loving the Son?

A. Because He redeemed us by His death.
4. Q. Why should you pray for the Holy Ghost?
A. Because He will sanctify us by His grace.

"Lord, thy glory fills the heaven;
  Earth is with its fulness stored;
Unto Thee be glory given,
  Holy, holy, holy Lord!

Heaven is still with anthems ringing:
  Earth takes up the angels' cry,
'Holy, holy, holy,' singing,
  'Lord of hosts, the Lord most High!'"

This last lesson should always be learned for the Sunday next before Advent.

THE CHURCH CATECHISM.

Q. What is your name?

A. N. or M.

Q. Who gave you this name?

A. My sponsors in baptism, wherein I was made a member of Christ, the Child of God, and an inheritor of the Kingdom of Heaven.

Q. What did your sponsors then for you?

A. They did promise and vow three things in my name. First, that I should renounce the Devil and all his works, the pomps and vanity of this wicked world, and all the sinful lusts of the flesh. Secondly, that I should believe all the Articles of the Christian faith. And, thirdly, that I should keep God's Holy Will and Commandments, and walk in the same all the days of my life.

Q. Dost thou not think that thou art bound to believe, and to do, as they have promised for thee?

A. Yes, verily; and by God's help so I will. And I heartily thank our heavenly Father, that He hath called me to this state of salvation, through Jesus Christ our Saviour. And I pray unto God to give me His grace, that I may continue in the same unto my life's end.

Q. Rehearse the articles of thy belief.

A. I believe in God the Father Almighty, Maker of heaven and earth, And in Jesus Christ his only Son our Lord; who was conceived by the Holy Ghost, born of the Virgin Mary, suffered under Pontius Pilate; Was crucified, dead and buried; He descended into hell; the third day He rose from the dead; He ascended into heaven; And sitteth at the right hand of God the Father Almighty; From thence He shall come to judge the quick and the dead.

I believe in the Holy Ghost; the holy Catholic Church; the Communion of Saints; the Forgiveness of sins; the Resurrection of the body; And the Life Everlasting. Amen.

Q. What dost thou chiefly learn in these Articles of thy Belief?

A. First, I learn to believe in God the Father, who hath made me, and all the world.

Secondly, In God the Son, Who hath redeemed me, and all mankind.

Thirdly, In God the Holy Ghost, Who sanctifieth me, and all the people of God.

Q. You said that your sponsors did promise for you that you should keep God's commandments; tell me how many there are.

A. Ten.

Q. Which are they?

A. The same which God spake in the twentieth chapter of Exodus, saying, I am the Lord thy God, who brought thee out of the land of Egypt, out of the house of bondage.

I. Thou shalt have none other gods but Me.

II. Thou shalt not make to thyself any graven image, nor the likeness of any thing that is in heaven above, or in the earth beneath, or in the water under the earth. Thou shalt not bow down to them, nor worship them; for I the Lord thy God am a jealous God, and visit the sins of the fathers upon the children, unto the third and fourth generation of them that hate Me, and show mercy unto thousands in them that love Me, and keep My Commandments.

III. Thou shalt not take the name of the Lord thy God in vain, for the Lord will not hold him guiltless that taketh his name in vain.

IV. Remember that thou keep holy the Sabbath-day. Six days shalt thou labour, and do all that thou hast to do, but the seventh day is the Sabbath of the Lord thy God. In it thou shalt do no manner of work, thou, and thy son, and thy daughter, thy man-servant, and thy maid-servant, thy cattle, and the stranger that is within thy gates. For in six days the Lord made heaven and earth, the sea, and all that in them is, and rested the seventh day; wherefore the Lord blessed the seventh day, and hallowed it.

V. Honour thy father and thy mother that thy days may be long in the land which the Lord thy God giveth thee.

VI. Thou shalt do no murder.

VII. Thou shalt not commit adultery.

VIII. Thou shalt not steal.

IX. Thou shalt not bear false witness against thy neighbour.

X. Thou shalt not covet thy neighbour's house, thou shalt not covet thy neighbour's wife, nor his servant, nor his maid, nor his ox, nor his ass, nor any thing that is his.

Q. What dost thou chiefly learn by these commandments?

A. I learn two things; my duty towards God, and my duty towards my neighbour.

Q. What is thy duty towards God?

A. My duty towards God is to believe in Him, to fear Him, and to love Him with all my heart, with all my mind, with all my soul, and with all my strength; to worship Him, to give Him thanks, to put my whole trust in Him, to call upon Him, to honour His holy Name and His Word, and to serve Him truly all the days of my life.

Q. What is thy duty towards thy neighbour?

A. My duty towards my neighbour is to love him as myself, and to do to all men as I would they should do unto me. To love, honour, and succour my father and mother; to honour and obey the civil authority; to submit myself to all my governors, teachers, spiritual pastors and masters. To order myself lowly and reverently to all my betters. To hurt nobody by word or deed. To be true and just in all my dealings. To bear no malice nor hatred in my heart. To keep my hands from picking and stealing and my tongue from evil speaking, lying and slandering. To keep my body in temperance, soberness, and chastity. Not to covet nor desire other men's goods, but to learn and labour truly, to get mine own living, and to do my duty in that state of life, unto which it shall please God to call me.

Q. My good child, know this, that thou art not able to do these things of thyself, nor to walk in the commandments of God, and to serve him, without his special grace, which thou must learn at all times to call for by diligent prayer. Let me hear, therefore if thou canst say the Lord's Prayer.

A. Our Father, which art in heaven, hallowed be Thy Name. Thy kingdom come. Thy will be done in earth, as it is in heaven. Give us this day our daily bread. And forgive us our trespasses, as we forgive them that trespass against us. And lead us not into temptation; but deliver us from evil. Amen.

Q. What desirest thou of God in this prayer?

A. I desire my Lord God our heavenly Father, who is the Giver of all goodness, to send his grace unto me, and to all people; that we may worship Him, serve Him, and obey Him, as we ought to do. And I pray unto God, that He will send us all things that are needful both for our souls and bodies; and that He will be merciful unto us, and forgive us our sins; and that it will please Him to save and defend us in all dangers both of soul and body; and that He will keep us from all sin and wickedness, and from our spiritual enemy, and from everlasting death. And this I trust He will do of his mercy and goodness, through our Lord Jesus Christ. And therefore I say Amen—So be it.

Q. How many sacraments hath Christ ordained in His Church?

A. Two only, as generally necessary to salvation; that is to say, Baptism and the Supper of the Lord.

Q. What meanest thou by this word Sacrament?

A. I mean an outward and visible sign of an inward and spiritual grace given unto us, ordained by Christ Himself, as a means whereby we receive the same, and a pledge to assure us thereof.

Q. How many parts are there in a Sacrament?

A. Two; the outward visible sign, and the inward spiritual grace.

Q. What is the outward visible sign or form in Baptism?

A. Water; wherein the person is baptized, *In the Name of the Father, and of the Son, and of the Holy Ghost.*

Q. What is the inward and spiritual grace?

A. A death unto sin, and a new birth unto righteousness; for being by nature born in sin, and the children of wrath, we are hereby made the children of grace.

Q. What is required of persons to be baptized?

A. Repentance, whereby they forsake sin; and Faith, whereby they steadfastly believe the promises of God made to them in that Sacrament.

Q. Why then are infants baptized, when by reason of their tender age they cannot perform them?

A. Because they promise them both by their sureties; which promise, when they come to age, themselves are bound to perform.

Q. Why was the Sacrament of the Lord's Supper ordained?

A. For the continual remembrance of the Sacrifice of the death of Christ, and of the benefits which we receive thereby.

Q. What is the outward part, or sign, of the Lord's Supper?

A. Bread and wine, which the Lord hath commanded to be received.

Q. What is the inward part, or thing signified?

A. The Body and Blood of Christ, which are spiritually taken and received by the faithful in the Lord's Supper.

Q. What are the benefits whereof we are partakers thereby?

A. The strengthening and refreshing of our souls by the Body and Blood of Christ, as our bodies are by the bread and wine.

Q. What is required of those who come to the Lord's Supper?

A. To examine themselves, whether they repent them truly of their former sins, steadfastly purposing to lead a new life; have a lively faith in God's mercy through Christ, with a thankful remembrance of his death; and be in charity with all men.

www.ingramcontent.com/pod-product-compliance
Lightning Source LLC
Chambersburg PA
CBHW020803230426
43666CB00007B/825